A Question of Consensus

A Question of Consensus

The Doctrine of Assurance after the Westminster Confession

Jonathan Master

Fortress Press
Minneapolis

A QUESTION OF CONSENSUS

The Doctrine of Assurance after the Westminster Confession

Cover image: Wikimedia Commons/London, Westminster Abbey, west façade

Cover design: Laurie Ingram

Library of Congress Cataloging-in-Publication Data

Print ISBN: 978-1-4514-6941-7

eBook ISBN: 978-1-4514-7235-6

The paper used in this publication meets the minimum requirements of American
National Standard for Information Sciences — Permanence of Paper for Printed
Library Materials, ANSI Z329.48-1984.

Manufactured in the U.S.A.

This book was produced using PressBooks.com, and PDF rendering was done by
PrinceXML.

For Elizabeth

Contents

Introduction

The nineteenth-century church historian William Cunningham once wrote an illuminating chapter on the doctrine of assurance in the teaching of the Reformers. Using the work of Sir William Hamilton as a foil, Cunningham made several basic points about the Reformation teaching. But it is the conclusion to his chapter that is of particular interest. Cunningham ends with a note about the controversies that have particularly surrounded the study of assurance:

> It is not easy to keep the exact high road of truth; and men, filled with some one important idea or object, are very apt to run into exaggerations or extremes. Upon no subject has this been more conspicuously the case than on that of assurance; partly, perhaps, because of the influence of Luther, Calvin, and their associates. It has happened repeatedly in the history of the church, that pious and zealous men, impressed with the importance of getting a larger share of attention to the subject of assurance, have been led into the adoption of untenable and erroneous positions concerning it.[1]

This may be an exaggeration, but if so, it is only a slight one. And it is not so surprising when we stop to consider the reasons. After all, the doctrine of assurance, which is the teaching about "the conviction

---

1. William Cunningham, *The Reformers and the Theology of the Reformation* (Edinburgh: Banner of Truth, 1989), 148.

or persuasion that one has been saved by the grace of God and is a Christian believer,"[2] cuts straight to the heart of the concerns of the Protestant Reformation, as well as those of everyday Christians.

In addition, a cursory look at the history of the Reformed churches in Scotland, which is not directly the focus of this book, would show that the controversy over assurance casts its shadow over much of the nineteenth century; indeed, it could be said that the Marrow Controversy was essentially a controversy about the necessity of assurance and the implications of it.[3] And certainly, the trial within the Church of Scotland of John McLeod Campbell revolved around the doctrine of assurance, even though the proximate cause of his deposition was his teaching on universal atonement.

In regards to the post-Reformation development in the area of assurance, Joel Beeke, author of several influential volumes on the post-Reformation doctrine of assurance, writes:

> Theologians and pastors of post-Reformation churches struggled for theological precision in defining the relationship between personal assurance and saving faith. Their labors produced a rich technical vocabulary that distinguished between assurance of faith and assurance of sense; direct (*actus directus*) and reflexive (*actus reflectus*) acts of faith; assurance of the uprightness of faith and of adoption; practical (*syllogismus practicus*) and mystical (*syllogismus mysticus*) syllogisms; the principle (*habitus*) and act (*actus*) of faith; objective and subjective assurance assurance of faith, understanding, and hope; discursive and intuitive assurance; immediate and mediate witness in assurance; and the being and well-being of faith. They used these terms within the context of related issues, such as possibilities, kinds, degrees, foundations, experiences, means, times, obstacles, qualifications, and fruits of assurance.[4]

2. A. T. B. McGowan, "Assurance," in *Dictionary of Scottish Church History and Theology*, ed. David F. Wright, David C. Lachman, and Donald E. Meek (Downers Grove, IL: InterVarsity, 1993).

3. Ibid.

4. Joel Beeke, *The Quest for Full Assurance: The Legacy of Calvin and His Successors* (Edinburgh: Banner of Truth, 1999), 1.

Beeke is certainly right about the precision with which many post-Reformation theologians wrote and spoke; clarity on the matter of assurance was a pressing pastoral concern and a key feature of a distinctively *Protestant* theology. Because of its distinctiveness, and because of the sometimes fine distinctions that characterized its expression, it should come as no surprise that, as Cunningham observed, "pious and zealous men, impressed with the importance of getting a larger share of attention to the subject of assurance, have been led into the adoption of untenable and erroneous positions concerning it."[5]

And yet, it is hard not to register some surprise at the state of affairs Cunningham observes. After all, the Westminster Confession of Faith, so central to the Reformed Protestant churches in the English-speaking world, speaks with remarkable clarity on the subject of assurance. It devotes an entire chapter to the subject. It devotes more than twice as many words to the topic of assurance as to the topic of saving faith (426 to 188). Even the nature of God and God's triune essence receives a mere 315 words. Now, to be sure, the number of words alone cannot give a measure of the topic's importance, but it can show that the topic was no mere afterthought. And indeed, while there was nearly complete consensus among those who held to the Westminster Confession on the nature of God and the Trinity, there has been wide diversity on the subject of assurance.

Some trace this diversity to the fact that Westminster got it wrong. The argument is that the Westminster Confession of Faith (WCF) went far beyond the Reformers themselves. We must give some attention to this proposal. But even if this were so (and, as we will see, it is not quite so simple), it still does not explain the wide diversity *after* Westminster *among those who agreed* with the WCF.

---

5. Cunningham, *Reformers*, 148.

In other words, regardless of the diversity of opinions leading up to the formulation of the WCF, and regardless of whether the WCF got the Reformers right, the fact remains that a great many people agreed with the WCF's relatively detailed statement on assurance yet disagree sharply with one another on the matter. How is this to be explained?

It is my contention that the diversity of opinion on the question of assurance can be seen almost immediately after the WCF was formulated. In looking primarily at three figures, each of whom agreed with the Westminster formulation in its entirety, and each of whom also shared to a great extent a common intellectual heritage and set of associations, we can see the beginnings of three distinct approaches to the question—three streams flowing directly from the headwaters of the Westminster Confession. Each stream has a way of answering the two main questions at issue in the debate: How can an individual receive assurance, and how can true assurance be distinguished from false? Each stream would grow and develop, leading to greater and greater divisions and innovations. The specific winding path of each stream is beyond the scope of this study; rather, what will concern us is the emergence of the streams.

The three figures I have chosen for this study are Anthony Burgess, Thomas Goodwin, and John Owen. Of the three, I spend the most time on Burgess, since he writes more extensively on the topic of assurance than the other two. I use Burgess in this study both to set the contextual categories with which we must be familiar (Puritanism, pastoral ministry, scholastic training) and to introduce the terms and categories of the debate. But in the end, all three are essential to our portrait, because, in looking at these three, we will see our three distinct streams emerge.

But to identify these streams, we must first understand the streams that led into the Westminster Confession of Faith. That means we must look at Calvin and Beza. In addition, we will have to try to understand the kind of document the WCF was and is—an effort that involves familiarizing ourselves with the process that led to its writing. Finally, we will need a thorough understanding of each of our major figures, including their backgrounds and associations, leading us to an understanding of what they said about the distinctive and debated topic of assurance.

This is a thorny topic, to be sure. But exposing the various ways in which the Westminster consensus was agreed with and then expanded upon should bring us somewhat closer to an understanding of the precise terms of which Beeke speaks, and the erroneous and untenable positions of which Cunningham warns. First, we must begin before Westminster.

1

Setting the Stage

Calvin, Beza, and the Reformed Doctrine of
Assurance before Westminster

Before we can address the Westminster doctrine of assurance or the
ways in which later writers interacted with and expanded upon its
formulation, we must look in general at the Reformed doctrine of
assurance prior to Westminster. This will be helpful for at least three
reasons. First, it will give us a better understanding of the kinds
of questions the Westminster Confession of Faith (WCF) was—and
in some cases was not—attempting to settle. Second, it will give us
a framework for comprehending the expansions on the consensus
reached at Westminster, which is our primary focus. Third, contrary
to the way in which the Reformed doctrine of assurance is sometimes
portrayed, the pattern of various streams of thinking within the
Reformed tradition on assurance prior to Westminster mirrors what
we will argue takes place after Westminster.

In this chapter, therefore, we will first give brief attention to the way in which John Calvin and Theodore Beza address the question of assurance. We choose these two because they are often seen as the most significant sources for the later English Puritan views, although it must be said at the outset that this conception is, as we will see, a significant oversimplification of the evidence. In the context of looking at Beza, we will also briefly attend to the question of the syllogisms. These syllogisms in particular must be addressed, in that they seem to provide the framework for much of what theologians writing after Westminster say on the question of assurance. Since using syllogisms to discuss assurance goes back at least to Beza, these must be introduced and examined here. Lastly, in this chapter, we must address the approaches that many scholars have taken to the question of the development of the Reformed doctrine of assurance prior to Westminster. As we will see, this has often been framed in terms of pitting the theology of Calvin against that of the English Puritans. We do not necessarily consider the question of Calvin versus the Calvinists to be among the most vital or helpful vantage points from which to view the historical evidence, and in fact, we would argue that it greatly oversimplifies the diverse views to be found on assurance in Reformed theology prior to the seventeenth century. Nonetheless, it is necessary to at least survey the ground from which so many scholarly salvos have been fired in order to place the present study in its proper context.

Calvin and Assurance

Many have questioned whether Calvin could assent to the first sentence of WCF 18:3, specifically the part that reads, "Assurance doth not so belong to the essence of faith." In apparent contrast to this, Calvin writes, "Now we possess a right definition of faith if we call it a firm and certain knowledge of God's benevolence toward us, founded upon the truth of the freely given promise in Christ, both revealed to our minds and sealed upon our hearts through the Holy Spirit."[1] The words *firm* and *certain* stand out particularly in Calvin's definition, as does the personal focus—it is "God's benevolence toward *us*." More than that, he writes that faith is "certainty, a firm conviction, assurance, firm assurance, and full assurance."[2] He writes, at greater length:

> Briefly, he alone is a true believer, who convinced by a firm conviction that God is a kindly and well-disposed Father toward him, promises himself in all things on the basis of his generosity; who, relying on the promises of divine benevolence toward him, lays hold on an undoubted expectation of salvation. . . . No man is a believer, I say, except him who, leaning upon the assurance of his salvation, confidently triumphs over the devil and death. . . . We cannot otherwise well comprehend the goodness of God unless we gather it from the fruit of great assurance.[3]

And again: "This so great an assurance, which dares to triumph over the devil, death, sin, and the gates of hell, ought to lodge deep in the hearts of all the godly; for our faith is nothing, except we feel assured that Christ is ours, and that the Father is in him propitious to us."[4]

Kendall, analyzing this evidence, writes, "The later distinction between faith and assurance seems never to have entered Calvin's mind."[5] He then goes on to say:

> That which Calvin does not do, then, is to urge men to make their calling and election sure to themselves. He thinks Christ's death is a sufficient pledge and merely seeing Him is assuring. Never does he

1. John Calvin, *Institutes of the Christian Religion*, 2 vols., ed. John T. McNeil, trans. Ford Lewis Battles (Philadelphia: Westminster, 1960) 3.2.16.
2. Ibid., 3.2.7.
3. Ibid., 3.2.16.
4. Ibid., 3.2.2.
5. R. T. Kendall, *Calvin and English Calvinism to 1649* (Carlisle, United Kingdom: Paternoster, 1997), 25.

employ 2 Peter 1: 10 in connection with seeking assurance of salvation. He regards 2 Peter generally as an encouragement 'to make proof' of one's calling 'by godly living' and 2 Peter 1: 10 particularly as an argument that our election is to be 'confirmed' by 'a good conscience and an upright life'. It should be noted moreover that Calvin does not link this verse to the conscience in terms of deducing assurance of salvation.[6]

We must therefore begin with an examination of what Calvin calls the 'certainty of faith.' Here is an extended quote from the *Institutes* that will perhaps provide some light:

> Here, indeed, is the chief hinge on which faith turns: that we do not regard the promises of mercy that God offers as truly only outside ourselves, but not at all in us; rather that we make them ours by inwardly embracing them. Hence, at last is born that confidence which Paul elsewhere calls 'peace' [Rom. 5:1], unless someone may prefer to derive peace from it. Nor it is an assurance that renders the conscience calm and peaceful before God's judgment. Without it the conscience must be harried by disturbed alarm, and almost torn to pieces; unless perhaps, forgetting God and self, it for the moment sleeps.[7]

While Calvin only mentions assurance in passing, it seems clear that "confidence" and "inward embrace" serve as useful stand-ins. Calvin seems to view assurance as something that is part and parcel of saving faith. It is hard to imagine someone having confidence of his or her salvation, along with a calm and peaceful conscience, without having assurance. Indeed, such a proposition seems almost nonsensical.

On other occasions, however, Calvin seems to strike a different note, as we can see in this string of quotations, also from the *Institutes*:

> Unbelief is always mixed with faith. . . . For unbelief is so deeply rooted in our hearts, and we are so inclined to it, that not without hard struggle is each one able to persuade himself of what all confess with the mouth,

6. Ibid. Kendall is quoting from John Calvin, *Commentary on 2 Peter*, preface and commentary on 2 Pet. 1:10.
7. Calvin, *Institutes* 5.20-21.

namely, that God is faithful. Especially when it comes to reality itself, every man's wavering uncovers hidden weakness. . . .

While we teach that faith ought to be certain and assured, we cannot imagine any certainty that is not tinged with doubt, or any assurance that is not assailed by some anxiety. On the other hand, we say that believers are in perpetual conflict with their unbelief. . . .

The greatest doubt and trepidation must be mixed up with such wrappings of ignorance, since our heart especially inclines by its own natural instinct toward unbelief. Besides this, there are innumerable and varied temptations that constantly assail us with great violence. But it is especially our conscience itself that, weighed down by a mass of sins, now complains and groans, now accuses itself, now murmurs secretly, now breaks out in open tumult. And so, whether adversities reveal God's wrath, or the conscience finds in itself the proof and ground thereof, thence unbelief obtains weapons and devices to overthrow faith.[8]

Here, Calvin does warn against basing one's assurance strictly on works, as when he writes, "For there is nowhere such a fear of God as can give full security, and the saints are always conscious that any integrity which they may possess is mingled with many remains of the flesh."[9] However, he can also write this with respect to the disciples in John 20:

There being so little faith, or rather almost no faith, both in the disciples and the women, it is astonishing that they had so great zeal; and, indeed, it is not possible that religious feelings led them to seek Christ. Some seed of faith, therefore, remained in their hearts, but quenched for a time, so that they were not aware of having what they had. Thus the Spirit of God often works in the elect in a secret manner. *In short, we must believe that there was some concealed root, from which we see fruit produced.* Though this feeling of piety, which they possessed, was

---

8. Ibid., 3.2.4, 15, 17, 20. Quoted and collated in Joel Beeke, *The Quest for Full Assurance: The Legacy of Calvin and His Successors* (Edinburgh: Banner of Truth, 1999), 42.
9. Calvin, *Institutes* 3.11.19.

confused, and was accompanied by much superstition, still I will give to it—though inaccurately—the name of *faith*, because it was only by the doctrine of the Gospel that it was produced, and it had no tendency but towards Christ. From this seed there at length sprang a true and sincere *faith*, which, leaving the sepulcher, ascended to the heavenly glory of Christ.[10]

Beeke summarizes the problem this way:

> How do we make sense of these seeming contradictions in Calvin? How can he say in one breath of many Christians, 'They are constrained with miserable anxiety at the same time they are in doubt whether he will be merciful to them because they confine that very kindness of which they seem utterly persuaded within too narrow limits . . .'—and then promptly proceed to add: 'but there is a far different feeling of full assurance that in the Scriptures is always attributed to faith . . .'?

> This prompts us to ask: How could Calvin say that assertions of faith are characterized by full assurance, yet still allow for the kind of faith that lacks assurance? The two statements appear antithetical. Assurance is free from doubt, yet not free. It does not hesitate, yet can hesitate; it contains security, but may be beset with anxiety; the faithful have assurance, yet waver and tremble.[11]

If we are to understand the context in which the WCF was formulated and the kinds of categories it was attempting to work within, we should understand something of these apparent contradictions in Calvin's thought. More precisely put, we should see the varying ways in which Calvin writes (and Beza along with him), ways that lend themselves to particular applications in the post-Westminster period of mid-seventeenth-century England.

Anthony Lane summarizes Calvin's view of works and assurance when he writes, "The argument from works may never be the primary ground of our confidence. This must be 'the goodness of

---

10. John Calvin, *Commentaries of John Calvin*. Reprint, 22 vols (Grand Rapids: Baker, 1979) 18:250.
11. Beeke, *Quest*, 44.

God,' 'the mercy of God,' 'the free promise of justification,' 'the certainty of the promise,' 'Christ's grace.'"[12] And Lane again: "Calvin recognized that our works can strengthen or confirm our confidence, as evidences of God's work in us, and that they are a test of the genuineness of faith. But once they become the primary ground of assurance a *de facto* justification by works has been introduced which will lead either to despair or to a false self-confidence."[13] For Lane, the issue in Calvin is distinguishing between a means of assurance and a *primary means* or *ground* of assurance. In Lane's estimation, works provide a means of assurance, but not one that is primary or foundational.

This seems to be borne out in a more thorough reading of the *Institutes*. Note, for instance, this reference in volume III: "In the meantime, believers are taught to examine themselves carefully and humbly, lest the confidence of the flesh creep in *and replace the assurance of faith*."[14] Here we see assurance as something already present in the life of the true believer; it is something that can be lost, to be sure, but it is essentially present in the normal, true believer. Later in the same volume, Calvin declares, "There is another kind of fear and trembling [Philippians 2:12], one that, so far from *diminishing the assurance of faith*, the more firmly establishes it."[15] Once again, we see the same pattern: assurance is something already present; it can be lost, but it is essentially there in the life of the believer.

In fact, what we find is that Calvin is most concerned with believers trying to deduce their salvation from the wrong sources. One longer quote will again make this point clear:

---

12. A. N. S. Lane, "Calvin's Doctrine of Assurance," *Vox Evangelica* 11 (1979): 32–54, quotations from 34–35.
13. Ibid, 35.
14. Calvin, *Institutes* 3.22 (italics mine).
15. Ibid., 3.35 (italics mine).

Now, in the divine benevolence, which faith is said to look to, we understand the possession of salvation and eternal life is obtained. For if, while God is favorable, no good can be lacking, when he assures us of his love we are abundantly and sufficiently assured of salvation. 'Let him show his face,' says the prophet, 'and we will be saved.' [Psalm 80:3 p.; cf. Psalm 79:4, Vg.] Hence Scripture establishes this as the sum of our salvation, that he has abolished all enmities and received us into grace [Ephesians 2:14]. By this they intimate that when God is reconciled to us no danger remains to prevent all things from prospering for us. Faith, therefore, having grasped the love of God, has promises of the present life and of that to come [1 Timothy 4:8], and firm assurance of all good things, but of such sort as can be perceived from the Word. For faith does not certainly promise itself either length of years or honor or riches in this life, since the Lord willed that none of these things be appointed for us. But it is content with this certainty: that, however many things fail us that have to do with the maintenance of this life, God will never fail. Rather, the chief assurance of faith rests in the expectation of the life to come, which has been placed beyond doubt through the Word of God.[16]

Two things can be noted in these formulations. First, Calvin did believe that assurance of faith was a normally integral part of faith itself; elsewhere in the *Institutes*, it is identified as part of "the living root of faith."[17] But it would be unjust to push this too far. For Calvin also seems to say that this assurance—present in the mind of the converted believer—can be lost or minimized. Therefore, while it seems correct to assert that, for Calvin, assurance was a part of saving faith, it is equally true to say that Calvin could and did conceive of believers losing part or all of the assurance they had—through either sin, lack of reverence for God, or perhaps, a failure to dwell upon the promises of God—in short, through lack of consistent faith. And, it also must be noted, as a further qualification, Calvin viewed assurance

16. Ibid., 3.41–42.
17. Ibid., 5.54.

as part of *any* exercise of faith, because it is the Spirit's work. It seems Beeke is correct in his analysis, which is worth quoting at length:

> Consequently, the Christian may be tossed about with doubt and perplexity when faith is not in practical exercise, but the seed of faith, implanted by the Spirit, cannot perish. Precisely because it is the Spirit's seed, faith contains and retains the element of assurance. The sense or feeling of assurance increases and decreases in proportion to the rise and decline of faith's exercises, but the seed of faith can never be destroyed. Calvin said, 'In the meantime, we ought to grasp this: however deficient or weak faith may be in the elect, still, because the Spirit of God is for them the sure guarantee and seal of their adoption (Eph 1:14; 2 Cor 1:22), the mark he has engraved can never be erased from their hearts.'[18]

Beeke suggests that Calvin's apparently contradictory impulses stem from his attempt to distinguish between a definition of faith and the practical experience of faith in the life of the believer.[19] Beeke writes, "In short, Calvin distinguished between the *'ought to'* of faith in its essence, and the 'is' of faith as wrestled out in daily life."[20] He quotes Calvin to support the notion that this tension is one readily recognized by Calvin:

> Still, someone will say: 'Believers experience something far different: In recognizing the grace of God toward themselves they are not only tried by disquiet, which often comes upon them, but they are repeatedly shaken by gravest terrors. For so violent are the temptations that trouble their minds as not to seem quite compatible with that certainty of faith.' Accordingly, we shall have to solve this difficulty if we wish the above-stated doctrine to stand. Surely, while we teach that faith ought to be certain and assured, we cannot imagine any certainty that is not tinged with doubt, or any assurance that is not assailed.[21]

---

18. Beeke, *Quest*, 43.
19. Ibid., 44.
20. Ibid., 45.
21. Calvin, *Institutes* 3.2.16-17.

Perhaps Calvin can be rightly understood through an awareness of the tension between the "wrestling" experience of faith in everyday life and the "ought to" definition of faith's essence. In this case, then, although Calvin formulates his doctrine of saving faith and assurance in some ways that initially seem at odds with the WCF, it may in fact be plausible to suggest that the authors of the WCF were addressing something very present in Calvin's writings, and even formulating their theology in ways consistent with strands of his. Yet it also seems quite possible to conclude that, within Calvin's formulation, there existed some tension and different areas of emphasis, as indeed we will see throughout the Reformed tradition more generally.

Although this very cursory summary may provide some help, what we stated at the outset must be stated emphatically again: It is simply an oversimplification of the evidence to suggest that the main question is whether or not Calvin, as a singular figure, agreed or disagreed with the Reformed theologians who followed. Letham is worth quoting on this: "Popular history focuses on a few key figures and tends to bypass others. A temptation always exists to concentrate on 'star theologians.' Calvin was certainly *primus inter pares*. For us, he may well have overwhelming interest for his towering theological genius. But we must remember the network of theological interaction which covered Europe and which meant that Calvin was simply one of a range of influences in the process of theological cross-fertilization."[22]

In attempting to shed some light on the views of Calvin, we are not, therefore, implying that the key question is, as Kendall puts it, whether or not Calvin would have agreed with the English Puritans. That is an interesting question in its own right, but raising it often

---

22. Robert Letham, "Faith and Assurance in Early Calvinism: A Model of Continuity and Diversity," *Later Calvinism: International Perspectives*, ed. W. Fred Graham (Kirksville, MO: Sixteenth Century Journal Publications, 1994), 358.

means missing the many ways in which there was diversity on the matter of assurance in Reformed theology, a diversity we will see exemplified again, even after the formal codification provided by the later Westminster Confession.

Assurance in Theodore Beza

While John Calvin is surely more prominent in the minds of most commentators today, and the differences between his writings and those of the later Reformed tradition have engendered the most significant contemporary scholarly debate, it is quite possible that Theodore Beza's formulations on the doctrine of assurance had a greater influence on the minds of the writers of the WCF.[23] For instance, Anthony Burgess's treatise on assurance begins with a quote from Beza that seems to set the agenda for the rest of the work in many respects.[24] In addition, we will see that Beza's way of framing the questions on assurance bear striking resemblance, not just to Burgess, but also to others of his time. In this respect, it should be noted that, while Burgess barely quotes from any of the early Reformers in his treatise on assurance, Beza is the exception. Further, in *Vindiciae Legis*, Burgess quotes from Beza more than Calvin—thirteen times, rather than ten.[25] In fact, he quotes Beza

---

23. See Muller's arguments regarding Beza's influence on Perkins in Richard A. Muller, "Perkins' 'A Golden Chaine': Predestinarian System or Schematized *Ordo Salutis?*," *Sixteenth Century Journal* 9 (1978): 69–81.

24. There is a lively debate about the nature and extent of Beza's modifications of Calvin's theology in general, not just on this matter of assurance. Some see him as overly rationalistic, thus turning from Calvin's Biblicism. At the other end of the spectrum are those like Beeke, who writes, "Generally speaking, Beza was unconditionally supportive of Calvin's theology." Quoted in Beeke, *Quest*, 73.

25. He quotes from Beza on pages 24, 78, 166, 207, 218, 227, 233, 238, 265, 268, 271, and 274; from Calvin on 5, 7, 41, 76, 85, 97, 133, 134, 193, and 239. See Anthony Burgess, *Vindiciae Legis, or, a Vindication of the Morall Law and the Covenants, from the Errours of Papists, Arminians, Socinians, and More Especially, Antinomians in Xxx Lectures, Preached at Laurence-Jury, London.* The second edition, corrected and augmented. ed. London: Printed by James Young, for Thomas Underhill

more than any Reformation figure besides Luther himself; Beza, in his treatise on assurance, quotes from Luther only to distinguish his views from the Lutheran ones.[26]

Beza's definition of faith deviates slightly from that of Calvin. For Calvin, as we have seen, faith consists of a sure and certain knowledge. Beza, however, writes this:

> The faith by which the sons of light are distinguished from the sons of darkness is not simply that which we call knowledge which is common even to the demons, by which one might know to be true whatever is contained in the writings of the prophets and the apostles, but besides that a firm assent of the soul accompanies this knowledge by which the person is able to apply himself as his own the promise of eternal life in Christ, just as if it was fully his and he possessed the thing itself.[27]

It is true Beza is using the term *knowledge* here in a different way from Calvin, who would not have agreed that bare conjectural knowledge about certain facts is not equivalent to saving faith. Yet Beza is explicit about this. In making a distinction between "knowledge," which could simply be factual and uncommitted, and "firm assent," he introduces an important distinction, one that would later influence both the Westminster divines and those who followed after them.

Beyond this difference, Beza in general seems much more interested than was Calvin in the implications of predestination for assurance in the believer's life; in fact, he indicated that this was his

---

... 1647.[25] See, for instance, *Spiritual Refining, or, a Treatise of Grace and Assurance Part I : Wherein Are Handled, the Doctrine of Assurance, the Use of Signs in Self-Examination, How True Graces May Be Distinguished from Counterfeit, Several True Signs of Grace, and Many False Ones, the Nature of Grace, under Divers Scripture-Notions or Titles, as Regeneration, the New-Creature, the Heart of Flesh, Vocation, Sanctification, &C. : Many Chief Questions (Occasionally) Controverted between the Orthodox and the Arminians : As Also Many Cases of Conscience, Tending to Comfort and Confirm Saints, [and] Undeceive and Convert Sinners*. London: Printed by Jo. Streater, for T.U., and are to be sold by Thomas Johnson ... 1658. 96.

26. see above.

27. Replace with Theodori Bezae, *Vezelii Volumen Tractationum Theologicarum* (Geneva: Eustathium Vignon, 1582), 1:678.

primary concern in addressing predestination.[28] Nonetheless, Beza is aware of the potential problems for assurance introduced by the doctrine of election, and he introduces an important solution to those problems:

> But whither may I flee for succor in the perilous temptations of particular election? Ans. Unto the effects whereby the spiritual life is certainly discerned, and so consequently out of election, like as the life of the body is perceived by feeling and moving . . . that I am chosen, I shall perceive first by that holiness or sanctification begun in me, that is to say my hating of sin and by my loving of righteousness. Hereunto I shall add the witness of the Holy Ghost comforting my conscience. Upon this sanctification and comfort of the Holy Ghost, we gather faith. And thereby we rise up unto Christ, to whom whosoever is given, is of necessity chosen in Him from afore all worlds.[29]

Beza ultimately points the believer to the promise of Christ for his or her assurance of salvation. The allusion to John 6 in his final sentence makes that much clear. But he is also clear that the sanctification of the believer can serve a very important function in assuring one of his or her status as a believer, elected by God for salvation.

In addition, the most significant distinguishing characteristic of this formulation is the way in which Beza cites *sanctification* as a proof of genuine assurance. Though Calvin may have hinted at this, he was much more concerned with showing the things that ought to be present in genuine faith, such as inherent surety. Beza, in contrast, uses the terminology of "gathering" faith from the evidence provided in sanctification. At the very least, we could say that Beza's focus seems to reflect on the actual *experience* of the believer struggling with his or her assurance.

---

28. Beeke, *Quest*, 73.
29. Theodore Beza, *A booke of Christian Questions and answers: Wherein are set forth the cheef points of the Christian religion*, trans. Arthur Golding (London: William Verne for Abraham Veale, 1574), 16.

Beza expresses this basic approach even more clearly in his confession, and even goes further. Not only does he continue to connect the experience of assurance with observations about one's sanctification, but he also connects all of this with the reality of God's sovereign election; while we earlier saw his recognition that the doctrine of election posed "perilous temptation," here he seems to solve the problems caused by this doctrine by making an appeal to the certain evidence of good works:

> Seeing that good works are for us the certain evidences of our faith, they also bring to us afterwards the certainty of our eternal election. Faith lays hold of Christ, by which, being justified and sanctified, we have the enjoyment of the glory to which we have been destined before the foundation of the world (Rom. 8:39; Eph 1:3-4). This is so much the more important because the world holds it in less esteem, as if the doctrine of particular election were a curious and incomprehensible thing. On the contrary, faith is nothing other than that by which we have the certainty that we possess life eternal; by it we know that before the foundation of the world God has destined that we should possess, through Christ, a very great salvation and a most excellent glory. This is why all that we have said of faith and of its effects would be useless if we would not add this point of eternal election as the sole foundation and support of all the assurance of Christians.[30]

Karl Barth, who saw a great deal of discontinuity between Calvin and Beza (and then the later Reformed writers) in their doctrine of assurance, recognized this fundamental truth about Beza's formations. In a longer description of Beza's understanding of faith, he addresses assurance in Beza specifically:

> The *second testing* [according to Beza] addresses the *subjective* side of the relationship. We have said that faith saves us from perishing. But *do we have this faith?* is Satan's objection. There are two responses to

---

30. Theodore Beza, *A briefe and pithie Summe of Christian faith made in forme of a Confession, with a confutation of al such spurious errors, as are contrarie thereunto*, trans. R. F. (London: Roger Ward, 1639), 19.

this. Firstly, we have the *'testimony of the Holy Spirit'* [*testimonium spiritus sancti*] (the principle of Scripture), which continually enables us to cry out undauntedly, 'Abba, Father!' Secondly, faith as the 'application of Christ' [applicatio Christi] is not without *'effect and power'* [*effectus et vires*], not without his bringing about the 'regeneration' [regeneration] or 'sanctification' [sanctification] of the person. Beza understands this to comprise three things. He speaks, first, of the *mortification'* [*mortificatio*] of the old person, the fundamental and effective setting aside of his existence. Then he describes its *'burial'* [*sepultura*], the 'continuation' [continuatio] and the 'increase' [progressus] or 'mortification' [mortificatio]. This is understood as the factual decaying and decomposition of the dead old person, which happens in the afflictions that come to us, in the 'exercises' [exercitationes] that we must undergo to tame our rebellious flesh, and finally in our bodily death, which ends the battle between flesh and spirit. The third moment of sanctification or rebirth is the *'resurrection of the new person'* [*resurrectio novi hominus*], the illumination, strengthening and tutoring of our intelligence, of our will, and of all our capacities through grace. The subjective presupposition to which we shall cling over against such testing is that we shall believe the testimony of the Holy Spirit, and practice, each of us on the basis of our calling, the use of the 'gift of regeneration' [donum regenerationis], which is inseparable from faith as the 'application of Christ' [applicatio Christi].[31]

Whatever Barth's personal conclusions about the direction that Beza takes, he does recognize that Beza's doctrine of assurance was directly tied to his understanding of sanctification in the Christian life. That is, as we have already noted, for Beza, the question of faith and assurance seems more directly related to his understanding of the struggles of the everyday believer than with more abstract questions about faith's substance. What Calvin made room for in his definition, Beza puts in a central position. Because of this, it is also the case that Beza spends a great deal more time on the practical matter of assurance than does Calvin. Although Calvin acknowledges the issue

---

31. Karl Barth, *The Theology of the Reformed Confessions*, trans. Darrell L. Guder and Judith J. Guder (Columbia: WJK, 2005), 117–18 (italics in original).

and even frames it in a way that can be fitted into the later Reformed categories, it is Beza, rather than Calvin, who discusses the issue with a depth of detail and a connection to practical pastoral concerns.

So for Beza, eternal election, far from actually posing an insurmountable problem for the attainment of assurance, actually is the grounds of assurance. Because Christ's salvation of specific individuals has been decreed, because they had been elected before the world began, then their salvation was sure. The good works that believers perform point them to the fact that these eternal realities are being worked out before their eyes; as they see their sanctification, they can have confidence of God's work in election, which in turn gives assurance about the stability of God's saving work in their lives. But note that, even for Beza, good works are not the sole means of assurance, nor are they even the primary ones. Although he points people to look at their good works as evidences of saving faith, their ultimate assurance is to be grounded in the promises of Christ and the electing action of God the Father.

Once again, however, we hasten to say that the particular view one has about Beza's notion of assurance may be less consequential for understanding later writers than some participants in the contemporary debate would imagine. There are diverse streams within Reformed theology on the matter of assurance leading up to the seventeenth century. While it is probably the case that Beza, more than any other post-Reformation theologian, influenced much of the later thinking on the English Puritans, particularly on the matter of assurance, it is far from clear that this influence was determinative or that it was exclusive. In fact, the evidence would suggest that no figure, Calvin included, had this kind of decisive influence over the seventeenth-century Puritan view, codified in the WCF.

The Syllogisms

However, it is worth noting that one of the central ways in which later writers worked through the issue of assurance was through two syllogisms. Although it is less clear what position Calvin took on the syllogisms, it is widely recognized that these played a role in the thinking of Theodore Beza, who built upon Calvin's theology in many important ways. Beza emphasized both of the syllogisms. Beeke quotes Graafland's summary of Beza in this regard: "To these acts Beza reckons, in the very first place, sanctification, which is begun in us and consists of a hatred of sin and a love for righteousness. Secondly, Beza speaks of the witness of the Holy Spirit, which encourages my conscience. It appears that these two acts of the Spirit are so clearly recognizable that they can form a ground which enables us to ascertain and be assured of our faith and election."[32]

The first of these syllogisms, the *syllogismus practicus*, or practical syllogism, goes something like this: *Major Premise:* Those who are regenerate evidence particular characteristics. *Minor Premise:* I evidence those same characteristics. *Conclusion:* Therefore, I am regenerate. There were generally several biblical texts on which the practical syllogism was founded. Among them are 2 Pet. 1:5-10; 1 John 2:3; 2:5; 3:14; and 5:2.[33]

There are two important points to be made about this practical syllogism. First, the Puritans were quite emphatic that it could not be separated from the work of the Spirit.[34] The second point, which almost goes without saying, is that great discernment needed to be exercised in compiling the proper substance of the major premise.

32. Cornelis Graafland*De zekerheid van het geloof: Een onderzoek naar de geloof- beschouwing van enige vertegenwoordigers van reformatie en nadere reformatie.* (Wageningen: H. Veenman & Zonen, 1961), p. 69, quoted in Beeke, *Quest*, 77.
33. Beeke, *Quest*, 134.
34. Ibid., 136.

That is, one must always ask the question: What *are* the particular characteristics of true regeneration? It was to this question, primarily, that Burgess turned.

The other central way of looking at assurance was known as the *syllogismus mysticus*, or mystical syllogism. As its name implies, it was decidedly more difficult to pin down. Petrus Immens was a Dutch preacher in the late seventeenth and early eighteenth centuries (d. 1720). He studied theology under Witsius. Although not directly part of the Westminster tradition, he provides this helpful formal definition of the mystical syllogism:

> The believer looking into the word of God, discovers therein what is declared with respect to the heirs of salvation, to wit, that they have fled for refuge to lay hold on the hope set before them; – that the hunger and thirst after the righteousness of Christ; – that God gives to them a new heart, by taking away the stony heart of their flesh, and giving them a heart of flesh; – that they love God with all their strength, and are inclined to follow after holiness, without which no man can see the Lord. He then examines with the strictest scrutiny his heart upon all these points; and the result is, that he finds that all these things, in a greater or less degree, his soul has experienced – and directly draws the delightful conclusion, "I am an heir of salvation."[35]

Richard Lovelace tries to define the mystical syllogism more succinctly as "direct assurance by the Spirit."[36] And one way of describing the distinction between these two syllogisms might be to say that one is primarily oriented toward external, observable evidence, while the other toward the internal—evidences that might be termed subjective.

These syllogisms are important for us to understand for at least two reasons. First, they show two different approaches to the question of

---

35. Petrus Immens, *The Pious Communicant Encouraged*, trans. John Bassett (New York: Isaac Collins, 1801), 1:95, quoted in Beeke, *Assurance of Faith*: Calvin, English Puritanism, and the Dutch Second Reformation (New York: Peter Lang, 1994), 162.
36. Richard Lovelace, *The American Pietism of Cotton Mather* (Grand Rapids: Eerdmans, 1979), 96.

assurance, which, as we will see, fit fairly neatly with the approach followed by some who wrote on the topic after Westminster. As we will see, the fault lines between the emphases of several of the later writers fall along exactly these distinctions. But secondly, and perhaps just as significantly, both of these approaches to assurance assume that a genuine believer may struggle greatly to attain assurance of faith, and that this struggle is not a sign, in and of itself, that his or her faith is not genuine. In effect, the use of either syllogism is based on an assumption that a full assurance of faith does not immediately and permanently accompany saving faith.

Conclusions on Calvin, Beza, and the Syllogisms

The debate about the relationship of the later Reformed writings on assurance to those of Calvin and Beza has become an important one in the quest to understand the development of the Reformed doctrine of assurance codified at Westminster, as we will see in looking at some of the recent scholarly discussions. From our brief overview of the work of Calvin and Beza, however, we can conclude three things.

First, we must conclude that Calvin did understand that faith, in its essence, needs to have some element of assurance to it. It was of the essence of faith to have certain knowledge of Christ's reliable promises of salvation for *you* as an individual. This emphasis accounts for most of his writing on the subject, and it seems he was most concerned to refute the notion that faith involves some kind of lower or different standards than does knowledge. This emphasis on faith being a certain knowledge led him to the conclusion that certainty or assurance about its substance was essential.

At the same time, we can also conclude that even Calvin recognized that an individual's assurance of faith could come and go. Because of the weakness of the flesh and the ongoing struggle against sin, the sin of doubt and unbelief could creep in. In that sense, the need for assurance was a genuine pastoral concern. Although Calvin does not devote as much attention to this pastoral reality as the later English Puritans, he does recognize it as an important matter.

Beza, in contrast, seems to have this focus in view much more clearly. Although he also sets out to define faith clearly, he spends a great deal of time and energy on explaining how this works itself out in the practical course of Christian sanctification. Throughout it all, he is careful to not make good works the grounds of the believer's assurance, though he does highlight, much more clearly than Calvin, their importance for renewing the believer to an assured faith. Divine election, far from being an impediment that compels him to unhealthy introspection, instead becomes a further means of assurance, giving the believer confidence that what God is working out through sanctification is connected to a broader, eternal plan.

This leads to the third conclusion we can draw from our study of Calvin and Beza. As we will see in the WCF and in the writings of those who followed, the emphasis of the Puritans was much closer to that of Beza than to that of Calvin in this matter. There are certainly statements in Calvin that fit with the later statements at Westminster. But it is also the case that the burden of Beza—to show the struggle for assurance and to connect it clearly with sanctification—is also the burden of the later writers of the seventeenth century. This will be seen clearly in Burgess's own employment of the syllogistic framework and in his extensive attention to the marks of sanctification from which one can deduce a firm assurance of faith.

Although the contemporary debate demands that we look at Calvin and Beza and the syllogisms, that does not mean Calvin and Beza provide the only means of understanding the views on assurance within early Reformed theology. In fact, as we have argued throughout, there were different streams in this regard.

The Contemporary Debate

Our brief survey has highlighted certain aspects of both Calvin's and Beza's doctrine, including Beza's use of assurance. Our tentative conclusion has been that we can see differing streams within the Reformed doctrine of assurance, even in the earliest figures in the Reformed tradition. We can see these in Calvin himself, and they are especially visible when one considers the contribution of Beza. The reason why we surveyed Calvin and Beza is that these two figures have been the subject of most of the contemporary scholarly debate as it relates to the English Puritan doctrine of assurance. Although one could profitably study the theology of the later Westminster Puritans apart from looking at the Reformed writers who preceded them, such a study would be ignoring much of the debate within the last fifty years in the field.

Needless to say, the development of the doctrine of assurance from the days of John Calvin to those of the Assembly at Westminster has been subject of much contemporary scholarly debate.[37] Since our study relates to the views of assurance of some who participated in the debates at Westminster, or at least agreed with their outcome, and then expanded upon the WCF shortly thereafter, these later views have a bearing on this scholarly debate. But before we present a specific context to these later writings, built upon primary source material, it will be useful for our study to survey the secondary source material related to the development of the Reformed doctrine of assurance, in order to show the various ways in which the topic has been addressed.

---

37. See, for instance, Letham, "Faith and Assurance," 355–84.

Calvin and the Calvinists

Generally speaking, the contemporary debate has been framed in terms of Calvin and the Calvinists. More specifically, it is framed in terms of the question regarding whether or not John Calvin would have either agreed or disagreed with English Puritans. As we have already stated and will state again more conclusively, this does not seem to be the most fruitful approach to the subject. Nonetheless, our survey of contemporary approaches is forced to address it.

R. T. Kendall and His Precursors

Since the late 1970s, questions about Calvin and the English Puritans and their distinct views about atonement and assurance of faith often begin with a reference to R. T. Kendall and his work on Calvin and the English Calvinists who followed after Calvin.[38] While Kendall's work created quite a stir—probably for a number of reasons, not least his clear and highly readable prose—his basic thesis about the English Puritans was by no means new, as we will see. Nonetheless, for the time being, because of Kendall's influence, his thesis will serve as an appropriate point of departure for our analysis of Calvin and the English Puritans in the latter half of this chapter.

In an unpublished dissertation submitted in 1961 to Duke University, William Chalker could already write, "It has become increasingly clear that the fundamental understanding of God which stood behind Calvin's writings and gave them their theological integrity was in a large measure lost in the transmission of his thought through his successors. Verbal and doctrinal similarities between Calvin and certain later Calvinists may no longer be permitted to obscure the fundamentally different spirits which guided each."[39]

---

38. R. T. Kendall, *Calvin and English Calvinism to 1649* (Oxford: Oxford University Press, 1979).

Since our focus in this study is specifically on the doctrine of assurance, Chalker is especially helpful in denoting the ways in which he views certain English Puritans moving away from Calvin in this area. Chalker attempts to show this disjunction in several facets of their theology. And while his examination is useful at points, it does not, as we will see, adequately take into account the differences between some of the doctrinal formulations postulated by Calvin (and the later Calvinists) and their often more nuanced comments on particular biblical passages. In addition to this, Chalker's thesis does not take into account the questions that Calvin was seeking to address, in contrast to those that preoccupied the English Puritans. Nonetheless, he does serve to remind us that the questions raised by Kendall were not new to him. In fact, the seeds of these questions can be seen much earlier.

If one were to go back even further, one would see the fundamental disjunction that Chalker posits between Calvin and the English Calvinists is rooted in earlier observations and assertions made in Leonard J. Trinterud's 1951 article on the origins of Puritan theology in general.[40] While Trinterud does not focus in particular on the doctrine of assurance, he does quite clearly make the case that English Puritanism was not nearly as dependent on the writing and thought of John Calvin as one might initially have expected, or as the scholarly consensus of the time would have it. This was probably a necessary and important corrective at the time, and Trinterud ably introduces the fact that the English Puritans were not so entirely dependent upon Calvin as some had assumed; in fact, they had other sources and sometimes other concerns altogether.[41]

39. William Chalker, "Calvin and Some Seventeenth Century English Calvinists: A Comparison of Their Thought through an Examination of Their Doctrines of the Knowledge of God, Faith, and Assurance" (PhD diss., Department of Religion, Duke University) 1961, 4.
40. Leonard J. Trinterud, "The Origins of Puritanism," *Church History* 20 (March 1951): 37-57.
41. See ibid., 32.

Karl Barth also posited a fundamental disjunction between Calvin and the later Puritan writers. To him, the Puritan view of assurance, codified in the Westminster Confession of Faith, was decidedly different from the view of assurance propounded by Calvin, and not for entirely mundane reasons of differing contexts or theological concerns. He wrote, "[The Westminster formulation on assurance] is an assurance that apparently requires so much verbiage because something about it is not quite right."[42] What was not quite right, in Barth's estimation, is a subject we will give greater attention to later in this study, but the basic fact that he considered the Puritan doctrine of assurance to be a departure from Calvin cannot be disputed. It may be said that Barth, like Kendall and others who followed, also posited that there was an imbalance in Puritan theology that shaped its departure from the purer biblical formulations of Calvin and others who had preceded them.[43] Though Barth's assertions about assurance and the Westminster formulation will be addressed later in this work, it is sufficient to say now that Barth's reading of the English Puritans, in terms of their motivation and their final formulations, is in the final analysis not entirely fair or tenable when the English Puritans are examined carefully.[44]

It could further be said that this notion of a Puritan departure from Calvin was hardly new, even with Barth and the others just mentioned. Perry Miller described the Puritans of the seventeenth century as having made "drastic alterations" to the theology of the Reformation.[45] Although Miller's thesis was connected most closely with the American Puritan movement of the seventeenth century, he

---

42. Barth, *Theology of the Reformed Confessions*, 144.
43. See the critique by Muller in Richard A. Muller, *After Calvin: Studies in the Development of a Theological Tradition* (Oxford: Oxford University Press, 2004), 63–80.
44. For later analysis, see chapter 4.
45. Perry Miller, *The New England Mind: The Seventeenth Century* (Cambridge, MA: Harvard University Press, 1939), 92.

surely also believed it to apply to the English Puritans with which they were so closely connected, in theology as well as practice. Going back further again, George P. Fisher wrote of the Covenant Theology of the Puritans, which "softened the rigor of Calvinistic teaching by setting up jural relations in the room of bare sovereignty."[46] For Fisher, the disjunction was still quite pronounced, but where Barth and Kendall posited a hardening in the Puritan movement (away from Calvin's pure Biblicism), Fisher actually sees something quite different; he sees the greater detail of full-orbed covenant theology actually tempering the "bare sovereignty [of Calvin]."[47]

So while we began our discussion by citing several significant quotes from Kendall's thesis, Kendall's approach to the theology of English Puritans was not entirely creative or new. Over forty years earlier, we can see the same kinds of observations made by those comparing the contribution of Calvin—particularly on the question of assurance—with that of the English Puritans of the seventeenth century who followed after him.

The Beza Thesis

By the late 1960s, several important scholarly works appeared that identified Theodore Beza as the primary culprit in this movement away from Calvin (whether for good or ill), particularly on the doctrine of assurance. Among the most prominent of these were ones by Brian G. Armstrong and Basil Hall.[48] Armstrong's work deals with

---

46. George P. Fisher, *History of Christian Doctrine* (Edinburgh: T & T Clark, 1896), 348.

47. Ibid.

48. Brian G. Armstrong, "Calvinism and the Amyraut Heresy: Protestant Scholasticism and Humanism in Seventeenth-Century France" (PhD diss., Madison, University of Wisconsin, 1969); Basil Hall, "Calvin against the Calvinists," in *John Calvin*, ed. G. E. Duffield, Courtenay Studies in Reformation Theology 1 (Appleford, UK: The Sutton Courtenay Press, 1966), 19–37.

Protestant thinking in France, but it posits a category of "Reformed Scholasticism," tracing it directly to Beza and distinguishing it from the thinking of Calvin. This "Reformed Scholasticism" was said to have greatly influenced not merely the manner in which the later English Puritans addressed theological questions, but also the approach they took to the doctrines of predestination, the atonement, and one's assurance of faith. Hall, while also placing the blame for the movement away from Calvin firmly at the feet of Beza, makes more direct assertions (as the title of his article indicates), stating that the English Puritans expressed an interest in casuistic questions, foreign to the thinking of Calvin himself. Holmes Rolston III follows along much the same lines as Hall in his much more heated and polemical book, *John Calvin versus the Westminster Confession*.[49]

Scholasticism?

The notion of Scholasticism is an interesting one, and it deserves careful consideration. As we have said, a strong case can be made that later writers were heavily influenced by scholastic modes of thought. For some of them, their educational background was steeped in the kind of syllogistic reasoning normally associated with the Scholastic movement. And as we will see when we come to examine the later writings ourselves, certain authors' reflections on assurance surely did follow a kind of syllogistic procedure. But Armstrong and Hall mean something different from that. They do not simply believe that the English Puritans used scholastic modes of reasoning to reach their conclusions, nor do they assert that the approach they take to presenting their work simply follows the typical contours of the academic discourse in which they were steeped; rather, it is said

49. Holmes Rolston III, *John Calvin versus the Westminster Confession* (Richmond, VA: John Knox, 1972).

that the kinds of questions they ask and they ways in which they formulate their theology departs from the text of Scripture, addressing questions that were fundamentally scholastic, implying too that they were foreign to the biblical text.[50]

Another related hypothesis that arose at the same time is worth mentioning. Philip McNair suggested, in his 1967 work, that Peter Martyr was in fact responsible for the shift away from Calvin. It was he, not Beza, who contributed to making the work of the English Puritans so different from that of Calvin himself.[51] McNair's overall conclusions regarding scholasticism are fundamentally similar to those we have surveyed already; what differed was his hypothesis regarding the source of these changes in theological method.

Finally, though he does not address the question of Calvin's relationship to the Puritan doctrine of assurance, we should note the work of Von Rohr, whose 1968 article deftly describes the connection between the English Puritan understanding of the covenant and their reckoning of assurance of faith.[52]

The scholarly consensus was not nearly so uniform in the 1970's, however. Other works followed slightly different lines, tracing the development between Calvin and writers that followed, but rejecting the notion of a fundamental disjunction between the two. These writers include Jill Raitt, John Patrick Donnelly, and W. Robert Godfrey.[53] While each of these was addressing a particular figure or movement, it is striking to note that they rejected the radical

---

50. See for instance, Basil Hall, in "Calvin Against the Calvinists."
51. Philip McNair, *Peter Martyr in Italy: An Anatomy of Apostasy* (Oxford: Clarendon, 1967).
52. John von Rohr, "Covenant and Assurance in Early English Puritanism," *Church History* (1968), 195–203.
53. Jill Raitt, *The Eucharistic Theology of Theodore Beza: Development of Reformed Doctrine* (Chambersburg, PA: American Academy of Religion, 1972); John Patrick Donnelly, *Calvinism and Scholasticism in Vermigli's Doctrine of Man and Grace* (Leiden: Brill, 1976); W. Robert Godfrey, "Tensions within International Calvinism: The Debate on the Atonement at the Synod of Dordt, 1618–1619" (PhD diss., Stanford University, 1974).

disjunction posited between Calvin and the English Puritans, opting instead for a hypothesis that is much more reflective of a gradual shift, in keeping with the differing ecclesiastical and historical contexts. Perhaps most significantly, they also began to countenance a more nuanced conclusion that posits neither total continuity nor total discontinuity, but rather several streams of thought within Reformed theology. In the end, this would become the scholarly consensus, and it is our conclusion as well.

Another important contribution to our understanding of the relationship of Puritan theology to the theology of John Calvin—particularly on the question of assurance—came from Robert Letham in his dissertation entitled, "Saving Faith and Assurance in Reformed Theology: Zwingli to the Synod of Dort."[54] In this 1979 work, Letham concludes that the Reformed doctrine of faith and of assurance actually has two distinct streams. Calvin, though the first among equals, was not the primary source that should be looked to in trying to understand the later Puritans. In fact, from the time of Calvin, two positions on faith and assurance existed. The two views of assurance can roughly be described as seeing assurance either as an essential part of saving faith or as a fruit of such faith, to be experienced subsequent to such faith. Letham's summary is worth quoting at length:

> Flowing from these two perspectives on faith are two divergent views of assurance of salvation. The first sees assurance as part of saving faith, as its essential, normative, definitive component. *Certitudo salutis* comes with faith and grows in step with it. The ground of assurance and the object of saving faith are therefore identical, being based objectively *extra nos* in the promise of God as it finds its focus in Christ. The second position sees assurance of salvation to be a fruit or effect of saving faith. While not necessarily intending to sever the organic connection

---

54. Robert W. A. Letham, "Saving Faith and Assurance in Reformed Theology: Zwingli to the Synod of Dort" (PhD diss., Faculty of Divinity, University of Aberdeen, 1979).

between the two, assurance is nevertheless understood to be a consequence of faith rather than a definitive component. Therefore, the ground of assurance and the object of faith are not precisely identical. While the object of saving faith is objective, being located in God's promise in Christ, the ground of assurance is normally subjective—*intra nos*—based on the perception of sanctification and good works in the one who exercises faith.[55]

In Letham's reckoning, these different ways of viewing faith and assurance were related to particular understandings of covenant theology, one that was held by Calvin, Zwingli, and Bucer (among others), the other of which was held by Bullinger, Tyndale, and Ursinus, spreading into the Netherlands and then in some respects back into England. His recognition of two distinct streams within Reformed theology allows him to take a mediating position on the question of differences between Calvin and the English Puritans. On the one hand, Letham agrees that the later writers say very different things than Calvin; on the other, he does not attribute this to one disjunctive figure who introduces a new scholastic tendency into Reformed thought.[56] This thesis is in a great many respects better than those that postulate a radical disjunction, and it rightly notes some diverse elements within the Reformed, while it does not spend a great deal of time considering the possibility of changing pastoral context. Of all the approaches surveyed, Letham's offers the most careful and balanced approach with respect to assurance.

The 1980s saw many new contributions to the topic emerge. The most notable of these came from Richard A. Muller. Muller's central insight, with respect to the question at hand, was that the theologians in the post-Reformation period often did use scholastic categories to expand upon the teachings established by Calvin and the other first-generation Reformers. But their appropriation of these categories

55. Ibid., 1:3.
56. Ibid., 4–5.

of thought and presentation did not mean the essential theological conclusions were changing. That is, Muller asserts that there was essential agreement between those (including English Puritans) who followed the Reformers and the Reformers themselves, most notably John Calvin.[57] Any apparent differences can be explained by changing contexts and changing modes of argument, rather than by fundamentally different views. Other scholars followed this basic thesis, though with nuances and particularities all their own.[58] Muller's thesis and his extensive work in following up with an examination of Calvin in his context seems quite sound. And in fact, we will see that it describes quite accurately the ways in which we see Burgess developing the Westminster consensus while remaining firmly in the tradition of Calvin and the earlier Reformers.

During this same decade, Paul Helm responded to the Kendall thesis directly. His brief work addressed Kendall's methodology in many important ways, concluding that the Kendall thesis was unfair, both in its reading of Calvin and in its use of the later Puritan sources.[59] He also criticized the way in which Kendall provided an overly simplistic account of the nature of doctrinal development, particularly how he applied this account to the question of the atonement.

Not long after Muller and Helm, M. C. Bell wrote *Calvin and Scottish Theology: The Doctrine of Assurance*.[60] Though much of the

---

57. See Richard A. Muller, *Christ and the Decree: Christology and Predestination in Reformed Theology from Calvin to Perkins* (Grand Rapids: Baker, 1987).

58. See, for instance, Donald W. Sinnema, "The Issue of Reprobation at the Synod of Dort (1618–19) in Light of the History of this Doctrine," (PhD diss., University of St. Michael's College, 1985); Martin A. Klauber, "The Context and Development of the Views of Jean-Alphonse Turretini (1671–1737) on Religious Authority," (PhD diss., University of Wisconsin, Madison, 1987); Stephen A. Spencer, "Reformed Scholasticism in Medieval Perspective: Thomas Aquinas and Francis Turrettini on the Incarnation" (PhD diss., Michigan State University, 1988).

59. See Paul Helm, *Calvin and the Calvinists* (Edinburgh: Banner of Truth, 1982); cf., Paul Helm, "Calvin, English Calvinism and the Logic of Doctrinal Development," *Scottish Journal of Theology* 34 (1981): 179–85.

new work of the 1980s was an essential rejection of the Kendall thesis, Bell's work was the opposite. Bell put forward the same thesis about Calvin and the Scottish theologians that Kendall had put forth for Calvin's relationship to the English Puritans. While Kendall's thesis dealt with the broader question of the atonement, which of course had implications for a doctrine of assurance, Bell's study focused simply on assurance, with the doctrine of the atonement providing the backdrop to this discussion. However, despite these superficial differences from Kendall's work, the basic conclusion was the same in terms of Calvin and the "Calvinists" who followed. He posited a severe disjunction between the two. And while it beyond the scope of this study to examine the particular nuances of Scottish theology and theologians, it can be said that Bell's work falls prey to the same basic methodological errors as does Kendall's; in fact, excepting the differences in geographical focus, their respective conclusions are remarkably similar.

In 1991, Joel R. Beeke's dissertation was published.[61] It, too, has shaped the debate in significant ways. In the last twenty years, Beeke has been among the most prolific writers on the subject of assurance, and it is to his more substantial work that we turn now.

Beeke asserts that the supposed disjunction between Calvin and the later Reformed theologians, whether in England or Holland, is in fact no disjunction at all. Beeke rather posits essential agreement between the two. In his reckoning, the differences can largely be attributed to several distinctive features of the later writers. First is their Trinitarian focus, which is to say they incorporate the doctrine of the Holy Spirit more explicitly into their formulations. Second is the pastoral context in which they ministered, which necessarily

60. M. Charles Bell, *Calvin and Scottish Theology: The Doctrine of Assurance* (Edinburgh: Handsel, 1985).
61. Joel R. Beeke, *Assurance of Faith.*

led them to give greater detail about the specific means for attaining assurance. The third feature was their scholastic categories. In this last reason, Beeke is following the basic contours of Muller's thought, and he does not delve too deeply into its implications. The first two distinctions (pneumatology and pastoral context) seem to frame most of Beeke's analysis.

Two important contributions, subsequent to Beeke's, should be noted as we try to understand Calvin and the English Puritans, particularly in the matter of assurance. The first is Richard Muller's monumental four-volume treatise on post-Reformation dogmatics.[62] Muller's project, begun but not yet completed when Beeke's work was published, is highly significant for several reasons. First, it is a remarkably detailed account of the ways in which Reformed orthodoxy solidified itself after Calvin. But more significant than that for our purposes is the fact that Muller is able to develop and prove his basic thesis regarding the methodology and substance of the later Reformed writers. He demonstrates quite thoroughly that the method of argumentation and presentation often changes between Calvin and the later Reformed writers, but that this change, even at the level of the questions being asked, was not a change in the essential substance of the doctrine that was affirmed. That is, Muller shows essential continuity between Calvin and the Calvinists, while at the same time providing a plausible and compelling reason for their apparent differences in approach. Because of the exhaustiveness of his research and the thoroughness of his presentation, it is hard to overestimate the importance of his work for our study. Muller also contributed to the discussion with his work on Calvin, especially *The Unaccommodated Calvin*, published in 2001.[63] Although neither

---

62. Richard Muller, *Post-Reformation Reformed Dogmatics*, 4 vols. (Grand Rapids: Baker, 2003).

63. Richard Muller, *The Unaccommodated Calvin: Studies in the Foundation of a Theological Tradition* (Oxford: Oxford University Press, 2001).

Muller's four-volume magnum opus nor his shorter studies of Calvin have a direct bearing on the matter of assurance, they do serve to undermine what appears now to be an overly simplistic reading of both Calvin and the Puritans by many who came before.

Along these same lines, a quite nuanced reading of Calvin's doctrine of saving faith emerges from the recent study by Barbara Pitkin.[64] Rather than limiting herself to the doctrinal writings of Calvin, especially the *Institutes*, Pitkin's work addresses Calvin's exegetical writings first, showing how his comments on the biblical text evidence a maturation of thought. This is a substantial improvement over earlier studies, and it seems that her work is a major step forward methodologically in the search for Calvin's full-orbed conclusions, incorporating more fully Calvin's exegetical writings.

Two more works deserve attention, although their contribution to the question of assurance is not nearly as substantial as some of the other books and articles we have surveyed. The first is a recent volume by Letham on the theology of the Westminster Assembly.[65] This book provides a very helpful survey of the both the historical and theological context in which the Westminster Assembly did its work. In addition, it also provides a summary of the doctrines expressed in the Westminster Confession of Faith itself. Letham's analysis of the question of assurance certainly takes the theses of Kendall, Barth, and others into account, and he is critical of Westminster's formulations on assurance in some important respects. (For instance, he sees the WCF formulation as contributing to a lack of assurance, rather than the New Testament emphasis on sure and certain knowledge.) Also, because he aims to set the assembly

---

64. Barbara Pitkin, *What Pure Eyes Could See: Calvin's Doctrine of Faith in Its Exegetical Context* (Oxford: Oxford University Press, 1999).
65. Robert Letham, *The Westminster Assembly: Reading Its Theology in Historical Context* (Philippsburg: P & R, 2009).

in its historical and theological context, Letham's book makes a worthwhile contribution to the discussion as a whole, though it should be noted that his overall comments on the Westminster formulation on assurance are rather brief. His book as a whole is a helpful synthetic work, bringing together the major doctrines of the WCF and attempting to set them in their historical context.

Lastly, Mark Dever contributed a rather sweeping critique of the Kendall thesis in his chapter entitled "Calvin, Westminster, and Assurance."[66] Although Dever makes some complimentary statements about the details of Kendall's work, his overall conclusion is that Kendall did not sufficiently take into account the difference in context between Calvin and the Puritans. Calvin was often writing in a polemical context against the prevalent Roman Catholic views, whereas the Puritans were writing over 150 years later to a people who had a national Protestant church to which they all belonged.[67] Dever argues, probably quite rightly, that these differences in context must be taken into account in order to allow these sources to engage in theological conversation with one another. It must be said, however, that while Dever's work is sensible and probably correct in terms of its overall approach to the sources, it does not break any significantly new ground in terms of sources or analysis.

Conclusion

In conclusion, it would appear that those arguing for a radical disjunction between Calvin and the later English Puritans have been refuted. At the same time, they have brought up some important points that should not be dismissed lightly. It seems that rather than

---

66. Mark Dever, "Calvin, Westminster, and Assurance," in *The Westminster Confession into the 21st Century*, ed. Ligon Duncan (Ross-Shire, Scotland: Mentor, 2003), 1:303–41.
67. Ibid., 341.

speaking of a uniform position of "Calvin" or "the Calvinists," we might better think in term of streams within the Reformed tradition, which, though broadly consistent, are sufficiently different because of their differing contexts to merit attention. In many respects, this approach to "streams" reflects the broad outlines argued for by Letham some thirty years ago—though, as his subject is beyond the subject of this study, I am not ready to affirm all the particular ways in which he sees these streams flowing. There are, as Letham argues, differences in emphasis; as Muller argues, differences in argumentation; and as Beeke argues, differences in ecclesiastical context between the first generation of Reformers, particularly Calvin, and the English Puritans who followed. In point of fact, the same phenomenon that we are here positing for Reformed theology after Calvin, along the lines of three contributions made by these writers, is the one we will argue for more vigorously for the period directly following the Westminster Confession of Faith. That is, there are differences in context and background that lead the divines to address assurance in very different ways, even while essentially agreeing on the Westminster consensus.

In addition, we would also add that our survey of both Calvin and Beza suggests that these streams are not difficult to discern even in the early writers themselves. Calvin especially seems to emphasize different aspects of assurance at different points in his writing. His commentaries contain emphases not found in the definitions he gives in the *Institutes*. Even the *Institutes* allow for greater latitude in interpretation than is normally admitted in the literature of Calvin versus Calvinism.

What is most interesting from the perspective of this study is the way in which these differing emphases and streams on the question of assurance in Reformed theology leading up to the seventeenth century seem to be mirrored by the differing streams we will see proceeding from the Westminster formulation itself. It is not that the streams themselves are all the same, but the fact of diversity is as much a part of the Reformed doctrine of assurance coming out of the WCF as it was going in. As we will see, the formulation at Westminster lent itself to differing understandings, and it is to this formulation and these differences that we now must turn.

2

———

The Westminster Consensus

The Westminster Confession of Faith (WCF) arose in distinctive political and theological circumstances. In fact, the theological and political backdrop to the WCF must be understood if the work of the assembly and its resulting Confession of Faith is to be grasped. Our first goal in this chapter is to set the Westminster Assembly and its Confession of Faith in its seventeenth-century context. Second, we will see why it is necessary to understand that the WCF is a consensus document, a conclusion we can reach more definitively in light of recent research on the assembly and its work. Third, we need to know something of the men involved in the debates surrounding it. We will particularly look at one participant, Anthony Burgess, because he plays such an outsized role in the remainder of our study. Finally, we will analyze and evaluate the debate on assurance and its outcome in the theological formulations of WCF chapter 18.

The Historical Background of the Westminster Assembly

The social and political events of the 1640s look more orderly in retrospect than they must have felt at the time. The events leading up to the Long Parliament, the formation of the Westminster Assembly, and finally, the writing of the Westminster Confession itself can appear inevitable, but we must remember that the upheaval that led to them would probably have seemed nothing short of earth-shattering for those involved.[1]

By any standard, the decade of the 1640s was a tumultuous time of change in England. Consider: In 1637, William Prynne's ears and face were brutally disfigured on account of his encouragement of Puritan practices.[2] Yet within four years, Puritan ministers preached regularly to groups of Parliamentary officials in Westminster Abbey.[3] Such a rapid turnabout is hard to envision, yet it speaks to the fundamental change that was happening throughout England, a change that was not merely a matter of who held power, but also to the very nature of the way in which government was to be conducted. As an example, the first act of the Long Parliament, which began in 1640, was to proclaim a public fast. This fast day included sermons by two Puritans: Cornelius Burgess and Stephen Marshall.[4]

Observers were not unaware of the religious dimension of the events leading up to the Long Parliament. One proclaimed in a speech, "Believe it Sir, Religion hath been for a long time, and is still the great design upon this Kingdom; it is a known and practiced Principal, That they who would introduce another Religion into the

---

1. For this basic insight into the events of the 1640s in England, I am indebted to the work of Larry Jackson Holley. See especially L. J. Holley, "The Divines of the Westminster Assembly: A Study of Puritanism and Parliament" (PhD diss., Yale University, 1979), 8.
2. John Spurr, *English Puritanism, 1603–1689*, Social History in Perspective (Basingstoke, UK: Macmillan; New York: St. Martin's, 1998), 94.
3. Ibid., 95.
4. Seaver, *The Puritan Lectureships: The Politics of Religious Dissent 1560-1662* (Stanford: Stanford University Press, 1970), 267.

Church, must first Trouble and Disorder the Government of the State, that so they may work their ends in a Confusion, which now lyes at the door."[5]

The convening of what was to become the Long Parliament was proclaimed by at least one well-known man at the time as the "cure-all Court of Parliament."[6] But Cornelius Burgess, in his fast day sermon, understood the "cure" to be rooted in changes to the church. In essence, Burgess suggested that in order for the problems of the nation to be redressed, the church needed to be reformed.[7] In particular, Burgess had in mind the restoration of sound preaching throughout England and the expulsion of aberrant doctrinal positions; in short, he exhorted the nation to enter into a special covenant with God.[8]

Marshall's sermon was aimed, not at the nation as a whole, but at Parliament in particular.[9] He exhorted Parliament to settle the religious debates that beset the Church of England; in particular, he was concerned with the influence of Roman Catholic practices, urging the members of Parliament to return to the basic principles of Protestant godliness. In his estimation, the stakes were high: if Parliament did not heed the call to address the matters of God before them, the nation would be ruined.[10]

So from the beginning, the Long Parliament was viewed, at least by some, as serving a religious function and owing a duty to the

5. Sir Benjamin Rudyard's Speech, 7 November 1640, in Rushworth, IV, 24. Accessed at http://www.british-history.ac.uk/rushworth-papers/vol4/pp1-45#h3-0267 on 3/1/15.
6. John Paget, quoted in Holley, "Divines," 9. The original citation Holley lists is John Paget, *A Defense of Church-Government Excercised in Presbyterriall, Classical, and Synodall Assemblies; According to the Practice of Reformed Churches* (London, 1641), n.p.
7. Cornelius Burgess, *The First Sermon preached to the House of Commons now assembled in Parliament at their Publique Fast, Novemb. 17. 1640* (London, 1641).
8. See ibid., 56.
9. Stephen Marshall, *A Sermon preached before the Honourable House of Commons, now assembled in Parliament, at their publike Fast, November 17. 1640. Upon 2 Chron. 15. 2* (London, 1641).
10. Ibid., 46.

reformation of the church. But a little over a month after the sermons of Cornelius Burgess and Stephen Marshall, these religious concerns came to a head with the introduction of the petition that came to be known as the "Root and Branch Petition."[11] Among other things, the petition called for the elimination of the episcopal government of the Church of England. It famously stated its demand that the episcopacy, "with all its dependencies, roots, and branches, may be abolished, and that the laws in their behalf made void, and the government according to God's Word may be rightly placed among us."[12] This petition had widespread support, having gained fifteen thousand signatures from the citizens of London and its surrounding environs.[13] Whatever one might think about the curative powers of parliament, it was clear that it would have to address questions of the English church at one point or another in order to accomplish the will of the citizenry. This is not, of course, to downplay the significant concerns that went beyond the theological, which are beyond the scope of this study, but it is to say that we miss one of the main thrusts of the Long Parliament if we forget that questions of religion and church reform were dominant from the start. Here Paul's warning serves us well in this respect: "If secular historians tend to under-estimate the importance of the Church and its theology in this period, Church historians are equally capable of ignoring the purely secular standards of action that the churches adopted to achieve their ends."[14]

By February 1641, an important step was taken by the Parliament. Both William Pleydell and Lord Falkland recommended that Parliament solicit assistance from theologians in order to handle the

---

11. Robert S. Paul, *The Assembly of the Lord* (Edinburgh: T & T Clark, 1997), 56.
12. S. R. Gardiner, *The Constitutional Documents of the Puritan Revolution* (Oxford: Clarendon, 1889), 67.
13. Paul, *Assembly*, 56.
14. Ibid., 7.

questions of church reform. Pleydell specifically requested that the House of Commons find "some Learned and approved Divines, who have spent their time in that noble Study."[15] Lord Falkland proposed a standing committee with membership taken from both the Houses of Commons and Lords. This committee would be made up also "with a number of such Learned Ministers as the Houses shall nominate for Assistants."[16]

Another very significant moment occurred in April 1641. The Scots, who had been presenting their concerns to Parliament in one way or another throughout the process, presented their demand for unity and conformity in religion between England and Scotland. This demand had been put off for some time in the interest of accomplishing other business, but it was highly significant when it was finally made.[17] A resolution was passed in Commons to approve of this request, and it was clear that the issues of church governance had to be resolved, not only to placate the desires of the citizens, but also to accomplish the important goal of peace with Scotland.

During the summer of 1641, the House of Commons took a few more mild steps toward instituting religious reform, but it was not until November 1641 (Parliament had reconvened on October 20 of that year) that the most significant step yet was taken. Article 185, known as the Grand Remonstrance, was written and presented to Charles I on December 1, 1641. It read, in part, "And the better to effect the intended reformation, we desire that there may be a general synod of the most gracious, pious, learned and judicious divines of this island; assisted with some from foreign parts, professing the same religion with us, who may consider of all things necessary for the peace and good government of the Church, and represent the results

15. William Pleydell, quoted in Holley, "Divines," 24.
16. Quoted in ibid., 24.
17. On the delay, see ibid., 30 n. 57.

of their consultations unto the Parliament, to be then allowed of and confirmed, and receive the stamp of authority, thereby to find passage and obedience throughout the kingdom."[18]

On December 24, Charles responded. Although on the surface he appeared to agree with the aim of the remonstrance, there were vagaries in his response that called into question his commitment to what was demanded.[19] At issue, among other things, was the question of who would select the members of this "general synod." On February 12, a parliamentary motion was granted stating, "Ordered, That on Tuesday Morning next, peremptorily, the Knights and Burgesses shall, respectively, bring in the Names of such Ministers whom they shall think fit to be employed for the Settling the Affairs of the Church: But first, that Day, Mr. Serjeant Wilde is to make Report of That Business from the Committee at Merchant Taylors Hall."[20]

On February 19, 1642, Commons again issued a grievance concerning the slow pace of church reform. Included in their proposed remedies were two important items:

> 14. That a due Reformation may be made of the Church Government and Liturgy, by the Parliament; and an able preaching Ministry established in all Parts of this Kingdom: To which Purpose they intend to be assisted with the Advice of such godly and learned Divines as shall be agreed upon by both Houses of Parliament.

> 15. That it may be established by Act of Parliament, that no Person shall incur any Penalties or Punishments, for any Omission of the Ceremonies in the Liturgy and Rubrick, until the intended Reformation be made by Parliament; and that such Ceremonies as are not established by Law may forthwith be wholly taken away.[21]

18. Quoted in Paul, *Assembly*, 59.
19. Holley, "Divines," 54.
20. "House of Commons Journal Volume 2: 12 February 1642," *Journal of the House of Commons*, vol. 2, *1640–1643* (1802): 427–29, available at http://www.british-history.ac.uk/report.aspx?compid=3332.

The key elements for our purposes are, first, the assistance of divines in reforming the church's government and liturgy and, second, that no one could be punished in the meantime for failing to comply with the ceremonies and liturgical practices of the national church. These were significant victories for the Puritan men; they were going to be given an opportunity to reshape the ceremonies of the English church, and they were going to be protected when, in matters of conscience, they dissented from the current strictures.

During these next months, Parliament was busy with other business beyond the reformation of the church. But the call for reform still was being issued forcefully. Cornelius Burgess was to play a pivotal role in this call. In a sermon preached on March 30, 1642, Burgess argued that the religious questions must be settled, notwithstanding the grave questions of military importance that were at stake: "In humane Reason, I confesse, they seem to councell wisely, who tell you that the Laws and Liberties of the Subjects must first be secured, before you fall upon Religion, which will do you little good, if, struggling for this, you be made slaves the while. But, Divine truth requires you to follow another method, first to build God's House, and to trust him with the building of yours, when his Work is done."[22]

According to Cornelius Burgess, time was of the essence:

> And yet, when all is done, you will be at length constrained to set upon that business, when the time will be more troublesome, your distractions greater, your oppositions stronger, your advantages lesse, your friends more disheartened, your enemies more strengthened, errors, Schisms, Heresies, and disorders more multiplied, and improved to the height of

21. "House of Commons Journal Volume 2: 19 February 1642," *Journal of the House of Commons*, vol. 2, *1640–1643* (1802): 441–45, available at http://www.british-history.ac.uk/report.aspx?compid=7626.

22. Cornelius Burgess, *Two Sermons, the First Sermon Opening the Necessity and Benefit of Washing the Heart; preached to Commons 30 March 1642* (London, 1645), 47.

impudence and threatening boldness: and yet, even then will you be compelled to break through all, and to conflict with whole Armies of those obstructions, which not you seem unwilling or afraid to set upon while they be single, or not so united as they will shortly be.[23]

Cornelius Burgess was arguing for them not to delay in summoning an assembly of divines. Though there were other quite weighty decisions before Parliament, this was one that could not wait. That same day, Simon Ashe preached a sermon arguing for much the same thing. In Ashe's case, though, he focused on the type of man that Parliament might call.[24] Ashe was concerned that the men appointed not be tinged with bias and that they be both intellectually and spiritually qualified for the task at hand.[25] On April 12, Parliament spoke with authority: "Ordered, That, on Tuesday next, the Knights and Burgesses of every English County shall bring in the Names of Two Divines; and of every Welch County, One; and of each University, Two; and of London, Four; to be consulted with, concerning the Government, Discipline, and publick Liturgy of the Church."[26]

On April 20, the first divines were approved by Parliament.[27] By May 19, the formal order was passed:

3a vice lecta est Billa, An Act for the Calling of an Assembly of godly and learned Divines to consult with &c.

Mr. H. Aiscough, of Yorke, B. D. and Mr. H. Robinson, of Leedes,

---

23. Ibid., 46–47.
24. For a discussion of this, see Holley, "Divines," 71.
25. Simeon Ashe, *The Best Refuge for the Most Oppressed, in a Sermon preached to the Honourable House of Commons at their solemne Fast, March 30 1642* (London, 1642).
26. "House of Commons Journal Volume 2: 12 April 1642," *Journal of the House of Commons,* vol. 2, *1640–1643* (1802): 523–24, available at http://www.british-history.ac.uk/report.aspx?compid=789.
27. "House of Commons Journal Volume 2: 20 April 1642," *Journal of the House of Commons,* vol. 2, *1640–1643* (1802): 535, available at http://www.british-history.ac.uk/report.aspx?compid=10018.

B. D. shall be named in the Act instead of Mr. Levitt, and Mr. Micklethwayte.

A Proviso was offered to be added: The which was twice read, viz. "As in their Judgements and Consciences they shall be persuaded to be most agreeable to the Word of God;" and, by Vote upon the Question, ordered to be inserted.

The Bill aforesaid, upon the Question, passed; and sent up to the Lords by Mr. Marten.[28]

One final piece of historical background is necessary in order to understand the work of the assembly. On September 25, 1643, a Solemn League and Covenant was signed between the English and Scottish Parliaments.[29] The covenant served a dual purpose. For England, Scotland promised soldiers to assist the English Parliament in their battles against the king; for Scotland, it promised Scottish representation at the Westminster Assembly and guaranteed that the differences in religion would be addressed in such a way that the two nations could achieve religious unity, "according to the word of God."[30] The Westminster divines now were not only charged with reforming the thirty-nine articles and the English church, but also charged with doing their work of reformation in such a way as to make it acceptable to the more international Reformed community, or at least compatible with the Scottish Presbyterians to the north.

---

28. "House of Commons Journal Volume 2: 19 May 1642," *Journal of the House of Commons*, vol. 2, *1640–1643* (1802): 579–80, available at http://www.british-history.ac.uk/report.aspx?compid=406.

29. The final form was printed as: *A Solemn League and Covenant, for reformation, and defence of religion the honour and happinesse of the King, and the peace and safety of the three kingdoms of England, Scotland, and Ireland. Also, two special orders: viz. I. Concerning the taking of the League and Covenant in all churches and chappels in London and Westminster, upon the next Lords-day in the afternoon. II. Concerning divers lords, knights, gentlemen, colonels, officers, souldiers, and others, that are desirous to meet this present Friday in the forenoon, at Margarets-Westminister, and to take the said League and Covenant. Die Sabbath, 30. Sept. 1643* (London: printed for Edw. Husbands, 1643).

30. For a discussion about the debate over this clause, see Paul, *Assembly*, 88.

While all of the members certainly wanted to see change, theirs was not a revolutionary mandate. Rather, the divines were charged with reforming something already in place (the thirty-nine articles) and trying to reach consensus with their Protestant neighbors.

The Assembly and Its Work

Having established something of the circumstances that led up to the formation of the Westminster Assembly, we now turn to the men themselves and to their work. We will see in general who they were and how they operated in debating the great issues thrust upon them.

Selection Criteria

Mitchell reports the somewhat overwrought assessment of Richard Baxter regarding the learning of the Westminster divines: "The Christian world since the days of the apostles had never a Synod of more excellent divines."[31] While it is true that they were quite learned and respected men within their circles, and most were seasoned pastors, the reality of their status is somewhat more complicated.

The House of Commons never specifically articulated the basis on which a nominee to serve on this assembly would be approved, prior to the signing of the Solemn League and Covenant. Holley has shown that one-third of the English divines held livings in or around London during this period.[32] Notwithstanding this outcome, it does seem to be the case that Parliament intended that two men should be chosen from each county. Richard Baxter affirms this, while acknowledging that some counties were un- or

---

31. Quoted in Robert Letham, *The Westminster Assembly: Reading Its Theology in Its Historical Context* (Phillipsburg, NJ: P & R, 2009), 33.
32. Holley, "Divines," 243.

underrepresented, "two were to be chosen out of each County; but some few Counties (I know not upon what reason) had but one; I suppose it was long of the Parliament men of those Counties."[33]

Holley attempts to analyze their makeup along economic lines, concluding that only ten percent were from poor families. He also notes that either sixty-four or sixty-six of the divines had published an independent work by June 1643.[34] Holley also notes, quite interestingly, that at least one-third (Holley actually believes this is a low estimate) of the divines had had run-ins with the law or with church courts.[35] However, as Van Dixhoorn remarks, "In most cases, sympathy to puritanism obtained among the nominees, but disaffection with Laud was no absolute requirement."[36] Still, Van Dixhoorn also notes, "Although not all were non-conformists, most of the divines invited were known to have been unhappy with one or more aspects of the Laudian regime."[37] In short, these men were basically nonconformists; all were well educated; their geographical distribution was intended to be broad; and patronage and friendships likely played a large role in their selection.[38] Although they shared many things in common—including a web of relationships and common causes—there needed to be a mechanism for reaching doctrinal consensus among them.

---

33. Richard Baxter, *Reliquiae Baxterianae: or Mr. Richard Baxter's narrative of the most memorable passages of his life and times* (London: Matthew Sylvester, 1696), 1:73.
34. Holley, "Divines," 156–65. Holley misses at least one, however: Anthony Burgess had a sermon published by this point!
35. Ibid., 169–70.
36. Chad Van Dixhoorn, "Reforming the Reformation: Theological Debate at the Westminster Assembly, 1643–1652" (PhD diss., Cambridge University, 2004), 1:30.
37. Ibid., 1:30 n. 76.
38. Van Dixhoorn writes, "At the end of the day, personal contacts or patronage may have been the most important deciding factor in the selection of divines by the knights and burgesses of each county. . . . A study of the friendships and patronage of these divines as a group is still wanting." Ibid., 1:29.

The Process for Debate

In addition to their plenary meetings, which as far as we know, always took place either in Henry VII's chapel or in the Jerusalem chamber of Westminster Abbey, the divines often met in committees to discuss issues about which they were to give a report.[39] The committees themselves, about which we have far fewer records, met in many locations. Lightfoot mentions meetings in other chambers, as well as one meeting in Edmund Calamy's house.[40] We also know there was ample opportunity for members to participate in whichever committee interested them, assuming that the committee a member began attending either finished its work or had reached a quorum without his presence. (The debate on assurance was begun, for instance, with the reading of the findings from committee three, the composition of which is unknown to us.)

The rules for debate were established on October 5, 1643. The assembly approved them and voted to be frequently reminded of them: "that these rules & the rules from the Lords and Commons should be read every Munday moneth & so it was voted."[41] Because of the recent discovery of the Lightfoot journal manuscript, we now have a detailed record of these rules. The rules were as follows:

Rules for the debates

1. That none speake but to the chaire[;] not till another sit downe.

2. The first stander up first heard unles some report be offered.

3. That Arguments of the Committee [be] first weighed before other be offered.

---

39. On the seating and the chambers for the plenary sessions, see ibid., 1:133–35, table 3.2.

40. From Lightfoot's MS Journal, fo. 13v Cambridge University Library, Dd.XIV.28(4), fos. 1r–62v. Quoted in Van Dixhoorn, "Reforming," 1:141.

41. From the Lightfoot Journal MS, discovered and transcribed by Van Dixhoorn, "Reforming," 1:173.

4. The point in question to be mentioned at the beg[inning] of each ones speech.

5. An argument in debate to be determined before more be offered.

6. All arguments answered before others be offered.

7. No rehearsalls [repetition or summary of other arguments – JLM] to be.

8. He hath not spoken shall be heard bef[ore] another that hath.

9. None speake against a vote without leave.

10. [A] violator of order to be interrupted.

11. Bef[ore] adjourning[,] concluded what to be handled the next session & at the session next[,] that order read.

For preventing absence

1. To come so earely as to sit at 9.

2. Where not company enough by 9 a clocke[,] the names to be called.

3. Prolocutor to note the neglecters generally without naming any & exhort that there be an amendment.

4. The common delinquents herein to be named Publickely.

5. Scribes keep a note of such.

For Committee

1. But 1 halfe & ½ hour for dinner time & then meet.

2. The orders in Committee observed as in assembly.

3. The same way for urging diligence in committee as in Assembly.

> 4. A member of severall Comittees stay in that Committee where he first comes till that committee be full & then to go[,] if he sees cause[,] to another.[42]

The committees met from Monday to Friday each week, with the exception of July 1643, when they also met on Saturdays. On the first Monday of the month, as stated in the guidelines, the rules were read. On the last Wednesday of every month, a fast day was held, with a sermon or sermons being preached that morning. All votes were cast by voice, and only a simple majority was needed to pass a motion. In the event of a tie, the prolocutor cast the deciding vote.[43] Committees alone were charged with producing documents, which would be presented as a majority report to the plenary session. The reports could then be debated or recommitted, as could the scriptural proofs offered. Eventually, though rarely that day, a vote would be taken on the whole measure.[44] Van Dixhoorn's quote on the final vote is significant, in light of the debate on assurance: "The final vote was important, for it required those who had dissented to parts of a document to express their views of the whole, thus putting their previous objections into a larger perspective."[45] The entire structure of the assembly was designed for a broad consensus. While the resulting document put to rest many significant debates, it ultimately reflected the wide agreement of the majority present; therefore, it did not put to rest all debate, nor was it designed to.

---

42. Transcribed and quoted in Van Dixhoorn, "Reforming," 1:173–74.
43. See, for instance, D. Meek, ed., "The Votes Passed Concerning Discipline and Government," in *The Works of George Gillespie*, ed. W. M. Hetherington (Edinburgh: Robert Ogle and Oliver Boyd, 1846), 2:3.
44. For more detail on these procedures, see Van Dixhoorn, "Reforming," 197–99.
45. Ibid., 199.

The Debate on Assurance

As the precipitating circumstances for the assembly would suggest, much of the work of the divines had to do with questions of worship, church order, and the relationship of the church to the state. The original mandate for the assembly made this focus imperative, and the Solemn League and Covenant, with the addition of the Scottish divines, only added to its necessity. But as we will see, the prolonged debate that took place around many aspects of the confession did not extend to the issue of assurance. In fact, it is striking to note how little debate seemed to ensue, bearing in mind that the divines were charged with writing a confession that would have far more than merely provincial significance.

Since the subject of assurance is one that the divines did not seem to spend much time debating, it is worth reprinting the deliberations in full. Essentially, as we will see, aside from the committee work (about which we know next to nothing specific to its work on assurance), the bulk of the assembly's work was completed between July 24 and 30, 1646. The final approval was on September 15 of that same year. Also included is an excerpt from the September 9 notes, which, although not directly concerned with the statement on assurance, surely overlaps in terms of subject matter. In our analysis, we will largely use the reconstruction provided by Van Dixhoorn:[46]

---

46. Van Dixhoorn's 2004 study is the latest and best attempt to reconstruct the minutes of the assembly. There are two parts to his study. The first is a straightforward 80,000-word thesis on the nature of debate within the assembly. However, in addition, Van Dixhoorn rediscovered and transcribed the manuscripts of John Lightfoot's journal, as well as the minutes of the assembly. These make up some six volumes of appendixes to his dissertation. In some respects, these transcriptions are still a work in progress, but nonetheless, the work thus far towers above earlier and less complete attempts such as those done by Mitchell and Struthers, and the rather incomplete editions of Lightfoot's memoirs that preceded Van Dixhoorn's rediscovery of the manuscript. All of these were consulted in the account recorded here, but in the end, Van Dixhoorn's work of reconstruction proved the most reliable. I am indebted to him for his personal help, as well as for his work in transcribing these important documents, which were critical in my understanding of the events of the Westminster Assembly. For the ongoing

Session 679: July 24, 1646: Fryday morning

Mr Wilkenson, Jn., Mr Woodcocke, Mr Guibon ware appointed to pray with the Lords, Commons and Committee of both kingdoms the weeke following.

Two Reports were made from the second committee.

Of certenty of Salvation, and of the state of the soule after death.

Ordered to debate the Report concerning the Certenty of Grace and Salvation.

The Assembly entred upon that Debate, and upon debate it was Ordered this to be the title, "of the certenty of Salvation."

Ordered: Although Hipocrates and other wicked men may vainely deceive themselves with false hopes and carnall presemptions of being in the favour of God and state of salvation <R[esolved] not to stand: and he has a spiders web>[47] (which hope of theirs shall perish), yet such as truly believe in the Lord Jesus and love him in sincerity, indeavoring to walke in all good conscience before him, may in this life be Assured that they are in the state of Grace, may know that they have eternall life, and that they dwell in Christ and he in them, and may rejoice in the hope of the glory of God which Hope shall never make them ashamed.

Resolved upon the Q[uestion]: This certenty is not a bare, morall, conjecturall, or probable perswasion grounded upon a fallible hope, but is an infallible <R[esolved]: not to stand "full">[48] assurance founded upon the divine truth of the promises of salvation.

---

work being led by Van Dixhoorn under the auspices of the Westminster Assembly Project, see www.westminsterassembly.org.

47. Interlined and circled in original.
48. Interlined.

Ordered to proceed in the debate.[49]

Sess. 680: July 30, 1646: Thursday morning

The Assembly proceeded in the debate wher they left and for the better connecting of the words following to those going before, for the clearing of some difficultyes in the debate, it was agreed to leave out the word "upon," and the mention of particular graces, and soe the words following are:

Resolved upon the Q[uestion]: these words shall be added to the former: The inward evidence of those graces unto which these promises are annexed, and the Testimony of the spirit of Adoption, witnessing with our sperits that we are the children of God, which spirit is the earnest of our Inheritance, wherby we are sealed unto the day of Redemption.

Ordered: This infallible certenty wher by a believer knowes himselfe to be in the state of Grace and Salvation, doth not soe belong unto the essence of faith as that a man cannot be a true believer or justified person without it.

Resolved upon the Q[uestion]: yet a true believer being inable by the sperit to know the things that are freely given him of God may without extraordinary Revelation in the Right use of ordinary meanes attaine thereunto.

Resolved upon the Q[uestion]: And therefore it is the duty of everyone to give all diligence to make his calling and election sure, that therby his heart may be inlardged in love and thankefullnesse unto the Lord in strength and chearefullnesse in the dutyes of obedience, and Inward peace and joy in the Holy Ghost.

49. Van Dixhoorn, "Reforming," 6:331–32.

Ordered: This Assurance of Salvation may severall ways in true believers be shaken, diminished and Intermitted.

Resolved upon the Q[uestion]: by negligence in preserving of it, by falling into some speciall sin, which woundeth the conscience and greiveth the sperit, by some sad <and>[50] heavy temptation, or by Gods owne withdrawing the light of his countenance, and suffering even such as feare him to walke in darkenesse and have noe light. Ordered: yet true believers are never utterly destitute of that seed of the sperit, and life of faith and love of Christ and of the brethren and conscience and duty, out of which this Assurance may in due time arise and revive againe and by the which in the meane time their sperit is supported from utter despaire.

Mr Palmer entred his dissent to the word "or" before "by Gods owne withdrawing."[51]

Sess: 700: Sept 9, 1646: Wensday morning

Resolved upon the Q[uestion]: "This faith is different in Degrees, weake or strong, may be Assailed with doubting, but gets the victory; cannot wholy faile or be lost, but at length obtaineth the end therof, the salvation of the soule, Christ the author being the finisher therof.[52]

Sess: 707: Sept 15, 1646: Tuesday morning

The Assembly debated the Report "of Assurance of Grace and Salvation" and upon debate it was Assented too, and is as followeth.[53]

---

50. Interlined in original.
51. Ibid., 6:333.
52. Ibid., 6:350.
53. Ibid., 6:355.

General Observation on the Deliberations

Several things become clear when reading through the record of the broader deliberations on assurance. Each is important to bear in mind when evaluating Burgess's later work on assurance, and indeed the broader work of the post-Reformation theologians and pastors to whom he might be compared.

First, it is clear that there was not too much debate on this issue. While there are not extant copies of the deliberations of the second committee on this, we do know that they spent some time on it; it was their report on July 24 that served to start the discussion and that largely seems to have been followed in the final work. However, within the entire assembly, there is a remarkable lack of interest in debating the specific proposals made by the committee.

This is not to say that the divines who were part of the assembly agreed on all the particulars regarding assurance. In fact, as we will see, there were some very significant differences—particularly when it came to the role of the Holy Spirit in sealing the believer.[54] These differences in approach to the Westminster consensus are a major part of our argument. But these differences were not pressed in the context of the debates in the assembly. What was agreed upon was uncontroversial at that time. The WCF statement was broadly agreed upon and little debated.

This in itself has several implications. First, it would seem to suggest that the relationship between the WCF and earlier Reformed formulations needs to be considered carefully. In essence, there are only a few options available in our analysis: First, the divines may have uniformly disagreed with Calvin or uniformly misunderstood him or not read him at all. These options seem unlikely, but they are at least hypothetical possibilities. Second, the divines may have

---

54. See chapters 4-5.

considered their writings on assurance to be beyond the scope of what Calvin was saying. That is, they were aware of Calvin's writings, understood Calvin aright, but saw him to be addressing different questions than they were addressing in their section on assurance.[55] What we surely know is that, for the men of the Westminster Assembly, the statement they agreed to regarding assurance provoked little discord or controversy. There was no large degree of tension on this matter. For our purposes at this point, it is enough to note that the divines did not see any reason for significant theological debate on the particular statement contained in the WCF.

That said, in addition to later disagreements that were not brought up in the assembly debates, there are significant areas of silence in the statement, or at least areas of suggestive ambiguity. The section on God's act of withdrawing assurance from the believer immediately presents itself: "Gods owne withdrawing the light of his countenance, and suffering even such as feare him to walke in darkenesse and have noe light."[56] Just what did that mean? How would it happen? Why would it happen? What were the pastoral implications of its possibility? All these questions are left unanswered. Another obvious example of silence regards the inward evidences of God's Spirit testifying to the believer's adoption. As we will see, this category of inward evidences will be highly significant in later writers. However, while it is mentioned in the statements produced by the assembly, it is not expanded upon in great detail. There is the question—so critical in Burgess's own later writings—of the means of gaining full assurance. Though the divines do mention the ordinary means and

---

55. We *know* that the divines were aware of and citing Calvin. For a representative example, Hoyle gave a speech on September 15, 1643, the substance of which centers around a quote from Calvin about God's protection of those who follow Him. See the minutes as transcribed in Van Dixhoorn, "Reforming," 3:95.

56. Ibid., 6:333.

also enjoin all believers to pursue assurance as part of their duty, there is a notable absence of teaching on how this is pursued.

The Deliberation on Assurance

One of the primary writers whom we will focus on in looking at the post-Westminster doctrine of assurance is Anthony Burgess. Burgess also had a role in the deliberations at Westminster itself. In general, we know that there was little debate on the topic of assurance. Because of the changing nature of committee assignments, we do not know precisely who made up the second committee, which was charged with bringing the initial proposal. More to the point, we cannot know precisely what Burgess's role in the debate was. But there are a few details that are worth noting.

Two comments in the minutes are worthy of mention in this regard. The first is from May 12, 1645. It relates to the formation of a committee to draft the confession:

Sess. 434. May [12] Munday morning

Debate about the committee for drawing up the confession.

The first draught of the confession of faith shall be drawn up by a committee of a few.

R[esolved]: the committee shall be 7.

Dr Gouge, Mr Reynolds, Mr Vines, Mr Tuckney, Dr Hoyle, Mr Herle, Mr Gataker [names circled in original]

R[esolved] Mr Gataker, Mr Reynolds, Dr Hoyle, Mr Herle, Mr Harris, Dr Temple, Mr Burges; they are to meet this afternoon [Herle,

Goodwin, Gouge, Burgess, Seaman circled, then Burges, Palmer erased.]

R[esolved] <Mr Burges [interlined]> for Mr Tuckney.[57]

Because of the various interlines and circles in the original manuscripts, it is quite difficult to be certain whether or not Anthony Burgess ended up on the committee. Van Dixhoorn is persuaded that Burgess was on the final committee, but we cannot be absolutely sure.[58] It does seem likely, given the final line of the resolution. In any case, we know he was among those considered best suited to the task. Of course, *if* Burgess was a part of the drafting committee, that underscores his importance in the whole debate.

Another fascinating episode comes from much earlier in the deliberations. The minutes for October 2, 1643, record a long debate relating to the topic of faith and works. This, of course, is closely related to the later discussion on assurance. Burgess plays a key role in the discussion:

Sess. 66. Octob. 2. Munday morning

Mr Bridge: *Fides quae viva non qua viva justificat:*[59] this is the scope of this place.

Mr Gibson: It is easier to know who hath not faith than who hath faith.

Mr Woodcocke: I question the proposition itselfe.

Mr Burges: He that questions that, next question that of our saviour, "by their fruites you shall know them."

57. Ibid., 6:117.
58. Ibid., 6:117 n. 8.
59. The meaning in English is something like "Living not as a living faith which justifies."

Mr Woodcocke: Christ speakes only of prophets, you shall know them by their fruites.[60]

The debate does not end after Burgess's statement, but it is clear where he stands. Genuine saving faith is shown by works. For Burgess, to deny this is to deny a clear statement of Jesus Christ. What is so striking about this is that it is one of the rare moments when Burgess is recorded as saying anything publicly in the full assembly. Van Dixhoorn singles out Anthony Burgess as *the* example of a divine who seems always to be at the heart of deliberations and is often appointed to committees of significant import, and yet who rarely says a word in the full assembly: "For example, Anthony Burgess utters only two recorded speeches (Minutes 1:81v; 3:203v), but he is often appointed to committees (Minutes 3:52v, 66v, 81v, 82r, 85r, 115v, 127r, etc.)."[61] The fact that one of the two times he speaks in the full group relates to this topic may be somewhat telling.[62]

Burgess was surely an active member of the assembly, although he was rarely vocal in its large-scale deliberations. He was likely part of the committee charged with drafting the WCF, though where he fits in the work of each specific committee is unclear.[63] Also, the one uninvited comment he makes is directly on the subject of assurance. His later work bears out this interest. We may not

60. Ibid., 3:133–34.
61. Ibid., 1:182.
62. The other time is when he was asked to give a report on March 29, 1647. His report pertains to John Orton's fitness for the ministry. After a weekend of evaluation, Burgess came back with the report of Orton, "He is a great malignant." The assembly agreed with his conclusion and concluded that they were "not satisfied concerning his fittnesse for that sequestration." Quoted in ibid., 7:164.
63. Although Casselli makes a significant point of assuming that Burgess was part of the third committee (and not the others), this does not appear to take into account what we now know about the way the committees functioned. Although Burgess *was* originally appointed to be on the third committee, we know that this was not a permanent assignment, and the divines frequently worked on committees other than the one to which they had been originally assigned.

know Burgess's precise role in the deliberations, but we know he was concerned about the matter of assurance that the Westminster Assembly discussed. While there was not great debate at the assembly on the topic, there were apparently matters that he felt required greater definition, and areas of silence that required greater articulation.

The WCF Theology of Assurance

Having looked at the most obvious elements of the debate surrounding the WCF statement on assurance and at Burgess's own role within the debate, we now must turn our attention to a detailed analysis of what the final statement itself actually says.

The Consensus

The consensus statement that the divines arrived upon has four sections. We have already seen above some of the statement in the transcription of the minutes, but the statement in its entirety is as follows:

> Section I. – Although hypocrites and other unregenerate men, may vainly deceive themselves with false hopes and carnal presumptions of being in the favour of God and the estate of salvation; which hope of theirs shall perish; yet such as truly believe in the Lord Jesus, and love him in sincerity, endeavouring to walk in all good conscience before him, may in this life be certainly assured that they are in the state of grace, and may rejoice in the hope of the glory of God; which hope shall never make them ashamed.

> Section II. – This certainly is not a bare conjectural and probable persuasion, grounded upon a fallible hope; but an infallible assurance of faith, founded upon the divine truth of the promises of salvation,

the inward evidences of those graces into which these promises are made, the testimony of the Spirit of adoption witnessing with our spirits that we are the children of God: which Spirit is the earnest of our inheritance, whereby we are sealed to the day of redemption.

Section III. – This infallible assurance doth not so belong to the essence of faith, but that a true believer may wait long, and conflict with many difficulties, before he be partaker of it: yet, being enabled by the Spirit to know the things which are freely given him of God, he may, without extraordinary revelation, in the right use of ordinary means, attain thereunto. And therefore it is the duty of every one to give all diligence to make his calling and election sure; that thereby his heart may be enlarged in peace and joy in the Holy Ghost, in love and thankfulness to God, and in strength and cheerfulness in the duties of obedience, the proper fruits of this assurance: so far is it from inclining men to looseness.

Section IV. – True believers may have the assurance of their salvation divers ways shaken, diminished, and intermitted; as, by negligence in preserving of it, by falling into some special sin, which woundeth the conscience and grieveth the Spirit; by some sudden and vehement temptation; by God's withdrawing the light of his countenance, and suffering even such as fear him to walk in darkness, and to have no light: yet are they never utterly destitute of that seed of God. and life of faith, that love of Christ and the brethren, that sincerity of heart and conscience of duty, out of which, by the operation of the Spirit, this assurance may in due time be revived, and by the which, in the meantime, they are supported from utter despair.[64]

---

64. Taken from A. A. Hodge, *The Confession of Faith* (London: Banner of Truth, 1958 repr.), 238, 242–43. They cite other verses for the entire statement, but for this clause, only one verse is enlisted in support.

Sections I–II

Section I of the chapter on assurance makes two essential points. The first of these is that there is a real possibility of false assurance. That is, there may be many who, although they are not truly saved, either presume or falsely hope that they possess salvation. It is noteworthy that this section does not explicitly outline the various ways in which this might take place: What might make individuals wrongly feel at ease in their state? What are the things that might be wrongly perceived as offering a sense of assurance? These are questions that would be of pastoral interest, but ultimately the WCF does not address them. The only hint the confession provides is in its employment of the phrase *carnal presumptions*. More specific guidelines were not given.

In light of Burgess's comment within the larger assembly about Jesus' own words, it is also quite interesting to note that the only biblical reference that the divines cite to buttress the phrase "which hope of theirs shall perish" is Matt. 7:22-23.[65] This is, of course, the same chapter that, just four verses before, contains the phrase Burgess cited in his aforementioned comment, "by their fruites, you shall know them." The verses that the divines do cite continue on the same theme, indicating that the false professors about whom Jesus spoke would not be saved in the end. Might this imply that the assembly agreed with Burgess that this passage does indeed speak clearly upon the matter of true believers and assurance? There is probably no way to know for sure, but it does underscore the extent to which Burgess's comment did indeed have bearing on the topic of assurance.

The second point about which section I of the chapter on assurance speaks clearly is the *possibility* of true and certain assurance. Now, this is not to say that this section suggests there is a *promise* of such

65. Quoted in ibid., 238 n. 2.

assurance, even for true believers. That type of promise is absent from the document, but the possibility of certainty is held out nonetheless.

On this second point, a more expansive explanation is given. The possibility of this certainty is held out in the case of those who sincerely love the Lord Jesus and who strive to walk in a good conscience toward him. This is not terribly specific, but it is certainly more specific than the first part of section I. For the believers seeking this kind of assurance, their satisfaction in their quest hinged would hinge upon their love and their obedience to the dictates of a pure conscience.

One cannot fail to observe, however, that the passages used to support this contention use somewhat stronger language than the confession itself. For the proposition that believers seeking assurance *may* have certainty, the references given are to 1 John 2:3; 3:14, 18, 19, 21, 24; 5:13.[66] With the exception of 1 John 5:13, these verses seem to hold out not just the possibility of assurance for the loving, obedient believer, but its actuality. This is a point that Letham makes about the final biblical text cited in section 1 as well, Rom. 5:2, 5.[67] Letham says, "However, [this statement about the possibility of certainty] is at odds with the apostle Paul; those who are justified by faith, while they suffer, *do* rejoice in the hope of the glory of God (Rom. 5:1-5)."[68] Indeed, if this absolute language is present in Romans 5, as indeed it appears, then it is also to be found in 1 John 2 and 3.

Section II builds upon the possibility envisioned in section I, that is, that a true believer with sincere love and a clear conscience may experience certainty of faith. Section II adds that it is not mere probability or hope in a vague sense; rather, it is an infallible

66. Quoted in ibid., 238 n. 3.
67. Quoted in ibid., 238 n. 4.
68. Robert Letham, *The Westminster Assembly: Reading Its Theology in Its Historical Context* (Phillipsburg, NJ: P & R, 2009), 286.

assurance. This possible infallible assurance is based, it seems, on two things: first, on the promises of salvation; second, on an inward testimony of the Holy Spirit. In this case, the witness of the Holy Spirit is given decidedly more space than the promises of salvation. The promises are only mentioned, but the internal witness of the Spirit is specifically cited as the "Spirit of adoption," "the earnest of our inheritance," and the means "whereby we are sealed to the day of redemption." To look at it another way, the clause regarding the promises of salvation is given merely one biblical proof, Heb. 6:17-18. The sentences on the internal witness have no fewer than eight passages and fourteen verses cited.[69] These citations not only raise questions about the relative importance in the thinking of the divines about these two means of assurance, but also raise particular questions about the interpretation of the passages in question. For instance, as we will see, there was a great debate following the assembly about the nature of the Holy Spirit's sealing ministry.[70]

Another glaring question emerges from this emphasis on the internal witness of the Spirit. Given the capacity for carnal self-deception about which the confession warns in section I, how is it that people can know objectively whether their internal sense of assurance is a result of the work of the Holy Spirit witnessing to their spirit or, rather, a "false hope and carnal presumption" on their part? From a pastoral perspective, this seems to be a very great question indeed. While the confession is clear that one can have an internal assurance that is entirely delusional, and while it is also the case that a believer *might* have an internal certainty that is entirely legitimate, how is one to discern the difference? As we will see, this exact question occupies much of the later writing on the topic.

69. The passages cited to support the notion of the internal witness of the Spirit are 2 Pet. 1:4, 5, 10, 11; 1 John 2:3; 3:14; 2 Cor. 1:12; Rom. 8:15, 16; Eph. 1:13-14; 4:30; 2 Cor. 1:21-22. Quoted in Hodge, *Confession of Faith*, 238 nn. 7, 8, 9.
70. See chapter 6.

Section III

Section III of the chapter on assurance is surely the most controversial in the contemporary debate. At issue is the question of whether or not the Westminster Confession is consistent with the views of Calvin in particular and the other earlier Reformers in general. Specifically, the question has been raised about the phrase "this infallible assurance doth not so belong to the essence of faith."[71]

Several observations must be made at this point. First, it is clear that the type of infallible assurance described in this section of the chapter must be defined by the sections that have come before. That is, the "infallible assurance" contemplated here is defined by sections I and II of the chapter. We cannot extract the phrase "infallible assurance" without acknowledging the "this" preceding it. All the observations one might make about the previous sections—a lack of specificity in certain areas, clarity in others—must be held in view when examining "*this* infallible assurance." This section does not stand in isolation, and we have already been told a great deal about its antecedent.

Second, it is striking to observe once again the emphasis placed on the work of the Holy Spirit in bringing this assurance. While the section does specify the use of ordinary means as the instrumental cause of the Spirit's work, what is in view is essentially still an internal sense, or "that thereby his heart may be enlarged in peace and joy in the Holy Ghost."[72] The assurance is something one feels, according to the WCF. In addition, it is brought about through a work of the Spirit and is therefore something best categorized as being in the realm of pneumatology.

71. Hodge, *Confession of Faith*, 242.
72. Ibid., 243.

Third, it is worth noting that the phrase *ordinary means* did require definition, even in the days in which the divines crafted this statement. While this section of the WCF contrasts "ordinary means" with "extraordinary revelation," that does not entirely settle the issue. In fact, as we have seen, defining the precise constitution of ordinary means was one of the primary tasks of the Westminster Assembly. Just what the ordinary means were and how they were to be actively pursued in the life of the ordinary Christian layperson were left unresolved in this statement. For pastoral reasons, if for nothing else, it would be left to others to explain and debate this issue more fully.[73]

Section IV

Although section IV does not refer to assurance with the adjective *this*, connecting it clearly with the descriptions of assurance given in the earlier chapters, it nonetheless seems most reasonable to conclude that this section is referring to the same phenomenon. Essentially, section IV makes two basic points. The first is that the assurance spoken of in this section may be severely damaged: "shaken, diminished, and intermitted."[74] The second facet of this section is related: that God will never allow someone who has experienced this infallible assurance to remain fully destitute.

This reinforces one of the points we have been making throughout: fundamentally, the type of assurance described by this chapter is one that involves an immediate inward feeling, in which the Holy Spirit ministers to the believer's heart, impressing upon him or her the reality of his or her salvation.

73. It should be noted, however, that the term "ordinary means" is used in Question 88 of the Westminster Shorter Catechism. There it is defined as "the Word, sacraments, and prayer."
74. Ibid., 243.

Summary and Conclusions

The Westminster Assembly was a meeting born of a crisis. The resultant confession was also a document born of a crisis. The crisis was the English Civil War of 1642. The causes of this conflict, as with any national event of this magnitude, were many and varied. From the perspective of Parliament, Charles I was acting in a manner that would essentially overthrow the Reformation—at least as it was understood by the English Puritans.[75] In addition, Parliament was concerned with an alliance with Scotland, which would have necessary religious implications. It should be noted that Morrill judges the Westminster Assembly to be a religious failure in achieving what he perceives to be its major objectives, namely, "the suppression of the Book of Common Prayer and its replacement by the Directory of Public Worship; the suppression of the old Christian festivals, particularly Christmas, Easter, and Rogationtide; the substitution of one pattern of admission to holy communion by another; the removal or destruction of idolatrous and superstitious objects and images from the churches."[76] Regardless of whether this assessment is accurate, it does underscore his previous assessment of the assembly as *the* significant response to *the* major precipitating factor of the English Civil War.

For the divines themselves, however, the assembly afforded the opportunity to address their own pressing questions. In addition to the larger political context of the Westminster Assembly, the divines used it as an opportunity to codify their own consensus on various issues of worship, church polity, and theology in general. They did so in a fashion that created the conditions for broad agreement, even among the many and varied individuals present at the deliberations.

75. Letham, *Westminster Assembly*, 28.
76. John Morrill, "The Church in England, 1642–9," in *Reactions to the English Civil War 1642–1649*, ed. John Morrill (New York: St. Martin's, 1983), 90.

They were responding to the theological needs of the day as they saw them. Many of these were in response to the developments within the established English church, and many by the need to robustly defend historically Protestant teaching.[77]

Further, the pastoral calling of the divines cannot be ignored. During the whole of their theological deliberations at the assembly, they were also acting very consciously as leaders within the church. Questions of ordination and the fitness of some individuals to minister were part of the regular work they undertook. Particularly when it comes to their statements on assurance, the pastoral context of the other divines must be borne in mind. Letham has even argued that the fact that most of the divines were working pastors explains their singling out the subject of assurance for special mention.[78] Beeke, too, recognizes that assurance is properly a pastoral concern. Indeed, at the end of his study of assurance in the post-Reformation period, he writes, among other things, "This study has shown the pastoral role of assurance."[79] Although he comes to vastly different conclusions in his analysis, Kendall, too, acknowledges the essentially pastoral nature of the formulations on the doctrine of assurance in the seventeenth century: "while Westminster theology, having been written entirely by pastors, is no doubt designed to encourage weak Christians."[80] While many of the gaps left by chapter 18 needed to be filled in by pastors for their flocks, it is nonetheless the case that the main points of the chapter are essentially pastoral in purpose.

And what did this lead to with respect to assurance? Many answers have been given to this question. Letham, giving one perspective,

---

77. This seems to be particularly the case with respect to soteriology. See John H. Leith, *Assembly at Westminster: Reformed Theology in the Making* (Richmond, VA: John Knox, 1973), 66.

78. Letham, *The Westminster Assembly*, 284.

79. Joel R. Beeke, *The Quest for Full Assurance* (Edinburgh: Banner of Truth, 1999), 281.

80. R. T. Kendall, quoted in A. T. B. McGowan, *The Federal Theology of Thomas Boston* (Milton Keynes, UK: Paternoster, 1997), 186.

summarizes the teaching of WCF chapter 18 by writing, "The chapter in the Confession presents assurance of salvation as very difficult to attain and extremely easy to lose—but cheer up, you will be kept from utter despair!"[81] Karl Barth, commenting on chapters 17–18 of the WCF, regards them as "truly a fortress of religious security based here on the consciousness of election, since neither the Catholic option of basing it on the church nor the Lutheran option of basing it on faith alone was possible."[82] Of chapter 18 in particular, he writes, "It is an assurance that apparently requires so much verbiage because something about it is not quite right."[83] Earlier in the same work, Barth calls the Westminster doctrine "reassurance," not assurance: "This intention of *reassurance*, which is profoundly pietistic and egotistic, is the worm in the timberwork, not the doctrine itself!"[84]

Letham's comment, while correct in its outline of the possibilities covered, seems to overstate the difficulty of gaining infallible assurance (as defined by the WCF) and also to overstate the ease of losing it. Although section III indicates that assurance may take a long time and be very difficult for a believer to attain, it is not something held out for only a few. It is not, for instance, something that requires special revelation, but rather hinges on ordinary means. In addition, though section IV countenances the possibility of losing this assurance (at least in large measure), it does not suggest that this is normal, probable, or even easy; it merely suggests that it may happen.

Regarding Barth's comments, it is questionable whether chapter 18 contains more verbiage than the others, and even more questionable that the language underscores some kind of evasion or confusion on

81. Letham, *Westminster Assembly*, 286.
82. Karl Barth, *The Theology of the Reformed Confessions*, trans. Darrell L. Guder and Judith Guder (Louisville: Westminster John Knox, 2005), 143.
83. Ibid., 144.
84. Ibid., 136.

the part of the writers. It is possible that they were all confused, but they do not seem aware of it, and their evasiveness is at best very well masked. Regarding Barth's main criticisms, which hinge on tone and perceived historical dissonance, two points must be made. First, it is far from clear that the assurance the Reformers referred to is identical to that spoken of by the divines of Westminster. On this possible distinction, two quotes from A. A. Hodge may be instructive. He writes, first, "Hence it follows that while assurance, in some degree of it, does belong to the essence of all real faith in the sufficiency of Christ and the truth of the promises, it is not in any degree essential to a genuine faith that the believer should be persuaded of the truth of his own experience and the safety of his estate."[85] Again, Hodge writes:

> Theologians consequently have distinguished between the assurance of faith (Heb. x. 22)—that is, a strong faith as to the truth of Christ—and the assurance of hope (Heb. vi. 11)—that is, a certain persuasion that we are true believers, and therefore safe. This latter is also called the assurance of sense, because it rests upon the inward sense the soul has of the reality of its own spiritual experiences. The first is of the essence of faith, and terminates directly upon Christ and his promise; and hence is called the *direct* act of faith. The latter is not of the essence of faith, but is its fruit; and is called the *reflex* act of faith, because it is drawn as an inference from the experience of the graces of the Spirit which the soul discerns when it reflects on its own consciousness.[86]

Something like this distinction may be helpful in analyzing this chapter. Regardless of the historical continuity or discontinuity between the Reformers and the divines at Westminster, what Barth calls "reassurance" and sees as profoundly "pietistic and egotistic" could better be understood using Hodge's rubric of the "assurance of hope."[87] It is far from certain that there was a technical way in which

85. Hodge, *Confession of Faith*, 244.
86. Ibid., 244.

the word *assurance* was always used in connection with salvation, set in stone by the Reformers and forgotten or ignored by the divines of Westminster.[88] This is particularly unlikely when one considers the broad consensus at Westminster about what finally made it into the WCF, combined with the breadth and depth of theological learning that the divines themselves exhibited.

Beeke, seeking to describe the broad outlines of WCF chapter 18, as well as its essential continuity with the tradition proceeding from Calvin, analyzes it in terms of what possibilities it envisions. He identifies three: false assurance, true assurance, and a lack of true assurance.[89] It is true that each of these is a clear implication of the wording of the WCF, though it must be said that the WCF does not explicitly state things in those terms. Nonetheless, Beeke, while avoiding some of the thornier issues in interpreting chapter 18, is essentially correct in his analysis. But the larger point for our purposes is that the pastoral implications of each of these possibilities are never fully explored in the WCF itself. And because these categories, correctly identified by Beeke, are inferences and not direct statements, putting the matter as clearly as he does requires some degree of post hoc analysis. However, we will see confirmation of Beeke's analysis of these three categories, borne out as they are in the later categories envisioned by Anthony Burgess, among others. But it should be noted that it is Burgess, and not the WCF itself, who makes these things clear.

What is abundantly clear is that chapter 18 left many holes to be filled. Whether the gaps were left to avoid debate and reach consensus is something we cannot know for sure. We do know that the rules

---

87. Ibid., 244. Barth quotes taken from Barth, *Theology of the Reformed Confessions*, 136.

88. For more on this distinction in the use and meaning of assurance, see also William Cunningham, "The Reformers and the Theology of the Reformation," in *The Collected Works of William Cunningham* (Edinburgh: T & T Clark, 1862), 1:131–32.

89. Beeke, *Assurance of Faith*, 148.

of the assembly were designed for just this kind of compromise. As it happened, in addition to the areas of silence, there were questions raised by this chapter that could hardly go unanswered.

In many important ways, we must conclude that the WCF statement on assurance reflects the consensus of the era—at least among the English Puritans and Scottish Covenanters during that day. Yet that consensus leaves open the precise ways in which its definition of assurance might differ from many who had used the term before. It also raises the question of how the ordinary means contribute to a greater sense of assurance. In what ways are these means to be employed in the life of a believer? How should the believer understand the role of the ordinary means when it comes to his or her absolute assurance of salvation? Especially when set against the backdrop of the major controversies of the day regarding church life and practice, this seems to be an area where greater clarity is required; it is also one to which Burgess speaks. And while the WCF lists some of the proper fruits of assurance, making it clear that assurance of faith leads not to "looseness," but rather to obedience and cheerful completion of Christian duties, in no place is this described as a comprehensive list; it does not seem intended to be exhaustive. But the lack of an exhaustive and authoritative list of the proper marks of an assured faith opened up wide possibilities for pastors seeking to understand how a properly assured faith works itself out in practice. Burgess later sees the need to devote a great deal of energy to addressing this silence.

It should also be said that not only did the WCF not address comprehensively the question of what marks true assurance, it also did not address in any measure the question of what does *not* constitute a mark of true and assured faith. If believers were to deepen their assurance, they not only needed to know what activities foster this—and what fruits are borne by it—but also needed to understand in some measure what things should not be taken as signs of genuine faith—that is, which activities and attitudes either are of no consequence at all in determining the state of one's soul or perhaps are even indications of counterfeit faith. Where the WCF is silent on this question, and many others besides, Burgess is manifestly not.

Then there is the overall question of what the WCF means when it describes assurance. Is this the same thing about which Calvin (for instance) spoke? Is Hodge's essential distinction between two types of assurance a fairer description than the radical disjunction (and devolution) postulated by Barth? And is Letham's concern over the pastoral implications of this doctrinal formulation borne out by the pastoral writings of the divines who agreed to the WCF statement? Burgess's later writings, in which he approaches the question of assurance in his own distinctive way, help us to answer these and other questions.[90]

The WCF was written in a time of great national and ecclesiastical upheaval. It had a particular purpose or goal, which in many respects, it admirably achieved. What it did not achieve is a final settlement on all the important pastoral issues related to assurance. In fact, its consensus statements in this regard actually opened the door for greater expansions to come. These expansions would be carried out by different people in different ways; in fact, there was no uniform approach to the issue even in the years immediately following the codification of the WCF.

90. Burgess's writings on these matters will be the subject of chapters 5–6.

3

———

Moving beyond Westminster

Anthony Burgess's Framework for Assurance

If Barth found the verbosity of the Westminster Confession of Faith (WCF) statement on assurance to be an indication that something was "not quite right," then surely the later writings by some of the Westminster divines would strike him as presenting an even greater problem. Anthony Burgess, for instance, expanded upon the WCF, filling in its gaps and silences, while staying within its basic framework. And he was not alone in these efforts. John Owen and Thomas Goodwin also considered the topic worthy of further verbosity.

Our method in this next section will be to examine the ways in which three key figures expanded upon the Westminster consensus, particularly in giving a framework for understanding true faith and genuine assurance. Examining these three will illustrate the fact that, while Westminster settled several issues with regard to the topic of assurance, it also left many significant things unsaid or unresolved.

Anthony Burgess gives perhaps the most comprehensive answers to the questions raised by Westminster, so we will begin with him in this chapter. But he does not give the only answers, and his answers will have to be seen in the context of others,' which we will discuss in chapter 5. In fact, when we examine these others, who approached the question of assurance in ways that would become highly influential, looking in particular at John Owen and Thomas Goodwin, we will see that their approach differed from Burgess's in quite significant ways.

These differences cannot merely be explained in the same way as the differences between Calvin and the later Puritans on assurance are explained—as stemming from pastoral needs or the peculiar contexts of national and religious life. Their differences stem from a different source. In fact, part of the historical methodology behind our selection of these three figures is precisely to control for possible differences in background, nationality, time period, and most importantly, familiarity with and adherence to the WCF. Though faced with the same kinds of pastoral challenges and gaps in the Westminster consensus, each of these three men expanded on the WCF in fundamentally different ways. These differences are surprising, given the overall agreement these figures would have shared with the WCF. Burgess, Owen, and Goodwin are roughly contemporary with one another; each would be considered a Puritan; each would agree with the Westminster consensus. Yet we will see in them different emphases with respect to the assurance of faith, providing us with different perspectives on the development of this important doctrine in the context of Reformed theology. We will begin in this chapter with Anthony Burgess and with the categories that apply equally to him, to Goodwin, and to Owen.

Anthony Burgess: Life and Background

Anthony Burgess's life and ministry took place at a significant moment, both in the history of England and in the history of doctrine in the English-speaking world. Richard Muller has referred to this period as that of "the rise and development of Reformed orthodoxy."[1] This description makes several important assumptions. First, it assumes that the Reformation was itself a watershed period in the history of Christian doctrine—an assumption that cannot reasonably be challenged. Second, it assumes that there are some basic structures to Reformed or Protestant thought that make up the core of its teaching. That is, whatever variants exist in the theology of Protestantism, they are precisely that—variants in an otherwise coherent system of thought. Notwithstanding this, Muller assumes that, within this basic framework, the period of 1520 to 1725 was one of development and codification within the basic tradition of Reformed or Protestant thought. Anthony Burgess (d. 1664) falls within this important developmental period.

In looking at Burgess and his contemporaries, we will contend that the contributions made to the doctrine of assurance must be understood within the framework of three categories. First, Burgess and the others must be understood as part of a movement within seventeenth-century England best labeled Puritan. Though defining this term precisely is notoriously difficult, it nonetheless provides useful shorthand for understanding the exigencies of the era and movement of which Burgess, Owen, and Goodwin were a part.

Second, each of these men must be understood in light of his pastoral calling. As we will see, the ways in which each expanded upon the Westminster doctrine of assurance are directly relatable to

---

1. Richard A. Muller, *Post-Reformation Reformed Dogmatics: The Rise and Development of Reformed Orthodoxy, ca. 1520 to ca. 1725*, 4 vols. (Grand Rapids: Baker, 2003).

pastoral experience and needs. Indeed, for Burgess, his treatises on assurance arise from a pastoral context. To ignore this is to ignore the driving force behind all that Burgess, Goodwin, and Owen write on assurance, and perhaps much of what they write on any theological topic at all. On this, those who have argued for comparing Calvin and the later Calvinists are quite correct: pastoral context makes a difference.

Finally, Burgess, Goodwin, and Owen must be understood broadly in light of a distinctive educational background. For Burgess, both his education in grammar school and his undergraduate and graduate education at Cambridge prepared and perhaps even predisposed him to particular ways of thinking and arguing. In fact, it could be argued that the distinctive education Burgess received during his formative years was actually the high-water mark for a peculiar kind of Scholastic method. Regardless, Burgess, as we will see, was a product of a distinctive training, and it is this training that shows us most clearly what he is doing methodologically as he expands upon the Westminster doctrine of assurance in his own distinctive way.

Puritanism

To begin our understanding of Burgess's contribution to the Westminster doctrine of assurance, we must first consider the term *Puritan*. Because of the scholarly debate regarding the meaning and usefulness of this term, it is perhaps the vaguest of the three designations we will use for description in this chapter.[2] But it is

---

2. For expressions of those who consider the term *Puritan* to be more or less worthless as a designation, see Paul Christianson, "Reformers and the Church of England under Elizabeth I and the Early Stuarts," *Journal of Ecclesiastical History* 31, no. 4 (October 1980): 463–84; J. C. Davis, "Puritanism and Revolution: Themes, Categories, Method and Conclusions," *Historical Journal* 33 (1990); Michael Finlayson, *Historians, Puritanism, and the English Revolution: The Religious Factor in English Politics before and after the Interregnum* (Toronto: University of

nonetheless important. Though the term *Puritan* itself needs some definition (it was used in different ways even in the sixteenth and seventeenth centuries), it appears to coalesce around certain shared emphases. Both Hill and Spurr agree, for instance, about the Puritan emphasis on the preaching of the Bible, Sabbatarianism, a particular view of home life, and in many cases, a willingness to emphasize these things even when it put those called Puritans on a crash course with the monarchy and the established church.[3]

One way to approach the problem is to see how the term *Puritan* was used when it first emerged in the sixteenth and seventeenth centuries. It appears most likely that the term began as a term of approbation. Udall writes in 1588, "I know no Puritans but Satan taught the papists so to name the ministers of the gospel."[4] In 1641, Henry Parker wrote that those criticizing Puritans are "papists, hierarchists, ambidexters and neuters in religion . . . court flatterers, time-serving projectors and the rancorous caterpillars of the realm . . . and the scum of the vulgar."[5] Parker also insisted that there were types of Puritans: church policy Puritans, religious Puritans, state Puritans, and moral Puritans.[6] And Parker again wrote, "Those whom we ordinarily call Puritans are men of strict life and precise opinions, which cannot be hated for anything but their singularity in zeal and piety."[7]

Writing somewhat later, Richard Baxter described the Puritans as "religious persons that used to talk of God, and heaven, and Scripture,

Toronto Press, 1983); Nicholas Tyacke, *Anti-Calvinists: The Rise of English Arminianism, c. 1590–1640* (Oxford: Oxford University Press, 1987); Basil Hall, "Puritanism: The Problem of Definition," in *Studies in Church History*, ed. G. J. Cumming (London: Nelson, 1965), 2:283–96.

3. See Christopher Hill, *Society and Puritanism in Pre-Revolutionary England* (New York: St. Martin's, 1997); and John Spurr, *English Puritanism 1603–1689* (Houndsmills, UK: Palgrave, 1998).

4. J. Udall, quoted in Hill, *Society and Puritanism*, 2.

5. Henry Parker, *A Discourse concerning Puritans* (London, 1641), 58–60.

6. Ibid., 13.

7. Ibid., 11.

and holiness."[8] A more comprehensive definition appears in the historical writings of Thomas Fuller from 1837:

> The English bishops, conceiving themselves empowered by their canons, began to shew their authority in urging the clergy of their diocese to subscribe to the liturgy, ceremonies, and discipline of the Church; and such as refused the same were branded with the odious name of puritans. . . . *Puritan* here was taken for the opposers of the hierarchy and church-service, as resenting of superstition. But profane mouths quickly improved this nickname, therewith on every occasion to abused pious people . . . that . . . labored for a life *pure* and holy. . . . These . . . were divided into two ranks: some mild and moderate, contented only to enjoy their own conscience; others fierce and fiery, to the disturbance of church and state.[9]

Fuller's description suggests that the term *Puritan* eventually came to describe a political movement. This does not seem to take into account the fundamentally religious character of the Puritan cause, though it does show that the movement came to have profound political implications. However, Fuller seems to create an artificial separation where none exists. Broadly speaking, in the sixteenth century, Puritanism described a group of people who wanted to promote the Protestant Reformation in England; in the seventeenth century, it became a party that tried to extend liberty and freedom against the British monarchy.

Although Puritanism was seen at the time and shortly after as a term that could be described with some coherency, it would be a mistake to think of it as a highly organized system or network. Brown, writing slightly later than Fuller, said Puritanism "was not so much an organised system (political or theological) as a religious temper and a moral force."[10] This would explain the diversity among

---

8. Richard Baxter, *Reliquiae Baxteriania,* (London, 1696), 154.
9. Thomas Fuller, *The Church History of Britain* (London: Thomas Tegg and Son, 1837), 4:327.
10. John Brown, *The English Puritans* (Cambridge: Cambridge University Press, 1910), 17.

those to whom the label is applied: there were Puritans both inside and outside the Anglican Church, and there were both Presbyterians and Congregationalists within the Puritan movement. So what united them? Brown suggests, "The fundamental idea of puritanism in all its manifestations was the supreme authority of Scripture brought to bear upon the conscience as opposed to an unenlightened reliance on the priesthood and the outward ordinances of the Church. . . . Under all its forms, reverence for Scripture, and for the sovereign majesty of God, a severe morality, popular sympathies and a fervent attachment to the cause of civil freedom have been the signs and tokens of the puritan spirit."[11]

Spurr offers a helpful, if slightly overwhelming, description of these various attempts at definition:

> Here the defining characteristic of Puritanism tends to be the immediacy and intensity of the individual's personal experience with God. Other historians, however, have offered more precise definitions, usually by identifying a particular characteristic of Puritanism. Thus, building on a long tradition, Walzer suggested that the doctrine of election bred anxiety and activism; Lamont saw a common thread in the pursuit of 'godly rule'; Nuttall dwelt upon the puritan's experience of the holy spirit [sic], while Coolidge emphasized their understanding of edification; McGee sought to distinguish the puritan from the Anglican by their different emphases on the two halves of the ten commandments; Lake has defined Puritanism as a set of priorities structured by religious experience, argued for a distinctly puritan, or 'experiential' appreciation of predestination, and suggested it was less individual beliefs and practices than the way in which they were combined that is typical of a puritan style; and Collinson portrays the puritans as the more evangelical protestants, whose identity stemmed in large part from their opposition to the luke-warm religion and profane society around them.[12]

---

11. Ibid., 17.
12. Spurr, *English Puritanism*, 3.

Christopher Hill, in analyzing this evidence, concludes that the term was used in different ways, even in the 1600s, which appears to be true, even from the evidence already cited. He prefers to categorize Puritans according to their emphases, which he sees as preaching, lecturing, industry, Sabbatarianism, discipline at all levels of society, treatment of the poor, oaths and interest, the family and household, and what might be termed various expressions of the church.[13] These, according to Hill, are, "some of the themes to which doctrinal Puritans attached importance."[14]

As it happened, the emphases of the Puritans put them at odds with Charles I. They were recognized at that time, and they recognized one another. It would seem Spurr and Hill are correct in at least assuming that Puritanism as a movement differed somehow in degree, if not always in kind, from that which surrounded it.[15] And as both of them noted and others seem to take for granted, it is striking to find that, while the seventeenth-century Puritans did not offer a clear and careful definition, they still seemed to recognize and associate with one another. That is, they seemed to recognize who could be considered a Puritan. Thus, although a precise definition may elude us, and a description of emphases and degrees of difference might be the best we can manage, it does seem to be a worthwhile designation.

No matter what definition is given to Puritanism in the context of seventeenth-century England, Anthony Burgess should be considered among its most significant figures. He fled his charge

---

13. Specifically, Hill refers to these as "The Preaching of the Word; The Ratsbane of Lecturing; The Industrious Sort of People; The Uses of Sabbatarianism; Discipline, Monarchical, Aristochratical, and Democratical; The Poor and the Parish; The Bawdy Courts; The Court of High Commission; The Rusty Sword of the Church; From Oaths to Interest; The Secularization of the Parish; The Spiritualization of the Household; and Individuals and Communities." Cf., Hill *Society and Puritanism,* "Contents."

14. Hill, *Society and Puritanism,* 15.

15. See also David D. Hall, "Narrating Puritanism," in *New Directions in American Religious History,* ed. Harry S. Stout and D. G. Hart (Oxford: Oxford University Press, 1997), 51–58.

prior to the days of the Westminster Assembly in order to escape persecution from Charles I. He was a part of the Westminster Assembly, was frequently asked to participate as the main preacher during the fast days of the Long Parliament, and suffered persecution in several forms—including, as we will see, ejection during the Uniformity Act of 1662.

So at minimum, it must be said that Anthony Burgess was an important theological figure at an important time in the history of doctrine in England. By any measure, from the narrowest definition to the broadest, he would be considered a Puritan—and a prominent one at that. In fact, I would argue that understanding the Puritan context of Burgess helps us place his writings in a political and ecclesiastical context. Burgess was not just a theologian, but a theologian operating within a certain constellation of pressures and figures in seventeenth-century England; his commitments and concerns were shaped by the other Puritans and the burdens they shared. In short, Anthony Burgess was an English Puritan.

Pastoral Ministry

One of the striking features of the seventeenth-century Puritan movement was the fact that it was led by pastors. It was not primarily an academic movement, although some of its main figures were involved in writing and publication. Indeed, notwithstanding the debate about whether it is a precise term, all would agree that the use of the term *Puritan* must denote a significant emphasis on preaching and pastoral work.

To illustrate this emphasis, let us turn to the first sermon preached at the convening of the Westminster Assembly, given by Oliver Bowles. Later it was published as *Zeale for God's House Quickened; or, a Sermon preached before the Assembly of Lords, Commons, and*

Divines, at their solemn Fast, July 7, 1643, in Abbey Church, Westminster: expressing the Eminency of Zeale required in Church-Reformers.[16]

However, while age may have been the motivating factor behind the choice of Bowles for the opening sermon, his choice of topic is no coincidence. Indeed, as the assembly progressed, the divines made it clear that the proper training and function of ministers was one of their primary concerns. This underscores the pastoral nature of the assembly's concerns and the assembly's preeminent interest in promoting zealous pastoral ministry within the church.

More than that, Bowles was an interesting choice because of his own particular ministerial focus. As P. G. Ryken argues, "[Bowles' work], *De Pastore Evangelico Tractatus* remains a major source for understanding the Westminster view of gospel ministry."[17] While many aspects of this work deserve special note, in this context it is especially relevant to understand Bowles's starting point for ministerial instruction: the personal godliness of the minister. He writes, for instance, about sexual sin, "because most gravely of all does the appearance or even trivial suspicion of this evil wound a man's reputation."[18] Bowles quickly follows with warnings against all types of worldly ambitions and greed, which can so easily ensnare.[19] The movement of which Burgess is a part was a movement that had, as its primary stated concern, a godly ministry.

So, for Burgess and those who were part of the seventeenth-century English Puritan movement, questions of pastoral theology

---

16. Oliver Bowles, *Zeale for God's House Quickened; or, a Sermon preached before the Assembly of Lords, Commons, and Divines, at their solemn Fast, July 7, 1643, in Abbey Church, Westminster: expressing the Eminency of Zeale required in Church-Reformers* (London, 1643).

17. Ryken, "Puritan Pastorate," 4.

18. This is a provisional translation of Bowles's Latin: "Quia omnium gravissime famam ejus vulnerat hujus mali spcies, vel levior suspicio." Bowles, *De Pastore Evangelico*, quoted in Ryken, "Puritan Pastorate," 4.

19. "Vel denique quibuscunque mundanis, quo minus ad coelestia animum attollat, irretitur." Bowles, *De Pastore Evangelico*, 26, quoted in Ryken, "Puritan Pastorate," 5.

were certainly not peripheral. Whatever else the seventeenth-century Puritans are known for (and Hill appears to be correct in his list of emphases), the ones whose theological writings we examine—and specifically, in this case, Burgess—must be seen in light of their work as pastors. The duties of a pastor were of significant concern, and the questions raised by congregations were near the center of his writings on assurance. Any attempt to discern why Burgess wrote so prolifically on the question of assurance must reckon with his pastoral background and context.

Since the Puritan movement was led by pastors and motivated by ecclesiastical concerns, it will be important for us to look more closely at the specific contours of Burgess's life as a pastor in order to better understand the kinds of congregational experiences that shaped his teaching. As we will see, Burgess's pastoral work was carried out in both urban and rural areas, during times of relative peace and stability and times of remarkable turmoil. Again, it will be contended that his pastoral calling is an essential lens through which to view his developments on assurance. So it is to the specific details of Anthony Burgess's life as a pastor that we now must turn.

Although the name Burgess has long been known to those who studied the period of the seventeenth-century Puritans, this was not because of Anthony Burgess, but is due rather to his collaborator on the Westminster Assembly, Cornelius Burgess. Cornelius Burgess was a kind of elder statesman at the assembly. Anthony, though revered enough to be invited—and often invited to preach on fast days as well—was not yet revered as highly. The confusion is exacerbated by the fact that Cornelius Burgess served as vicar of the church in which Anthony Burgess grew up.[20] Indeed, three Burgesses were part of the Westminster Assembly, and two of them, Drs.

---

20. William Barker, *Puritan Profiles* (Fern, Ross-shire, Scotland: Christian Focus, 1996), 26.

Cornelius and John Burgess, were ministers in the town of Watford, Hertfordshire, where Anthony Burgess was raised.[21] Cornelius Burgess was one of two assessors during the Westminster Assembly, which meant he was a kind of vice president, who chaired the assembly when William Twisse could not.[22] He was among the most widely cited figures in the minutes of the assembly and clearly one of its more prominent members. In any case, what must be noted at the outset is that Cornelius Burgess and Anthony Burgess were not related.

Anthony Burgess was an important and experienced figure in his own right, at least by the middle of the seventeenth century. In 1634–1635, Anthony Burgess was elected to serve as curate and lecturer at St. Mary Magdalen, Milk Street, London.[23] This was to be short-lived. Seaver summarizes: "Anthony Burgess, a Fellow of Emmanuel, having failed to secure a preaching license and admission to the curacy of St. Mary Magdalen Milk Street, was forced to give up his lectureship there after a month. Before the year was out he was admitted to the living at Sutton Coldfield, Warwickshire, and in 1643, when he returned to London as a member of the Westminster Assembly, he was promptly elected vicar of St. Lawrence Jewry."[24]

Sutton Coldfield, which Seaver also mentions in his summary, was a relatively small rural village. It had a significant Roman Catholic population, and according to Hughes, "Protestantism in the seventeenth-century Warwickshire had a rather conformist public face."[25] Hughes also notes that by 1642, "Puritanism had not been crushed, but its adherents had become all too aware of the dangers

---

21. James Reid, *Memoirs of the Lives and Writings of Those Eminent Divines Who Convened in the Famous Assembly at Westminister, in the Seventeenth Century*, 2 vols. (Paisley: Stephen and Andrew Young, 1811).

22. Barker, *Puritan Profiles*, 25.

23. Paul S. Seaver, quoting Guildhall Library Manuscript 2597/1, pp. 37, 49, in *Puritan Lectureships: The Politics of Religious Dissent 1560–1662* (Stanford: Stanford University Press, 1970), 256.

24. Seaver, *Puritan Lectureships*, 256.

of Episcopal repression, and conscious that they were living on borrowed time."[26]

As already mentioned, it was in October 1642 that Burgess fled to Coventry for safety.[27] He did so, "learning of the gathering of Royalist supporters at Kingstanding to welcome King Charles I."[28] This time in Coventry proved significant in Burgess's life. Coventry was, according to Hughes, favorably compared to Geneva, and the prevailing view was one of a "sternly disciplined Puritanism."[29] Every morning began with a lecture, in which Burgess often participated. It was from Warwickshire that Burgess was appointed a delegate to the Westminster Assembly in 1643.

Also, as we know, during his time in London, he also devoted himself to pastoral work. On January 25, 1645, he took over as vicar for the Guildhall Church, St. Lawrence Jewry, London.[30] After finishing his work with the assembly, he returned to his charge in Sutton Coldfield in 1649. This was to be his last pastoral charge. He was ejected for nonconformity in 1662.[31] Edmund Calamy wrote this about his ejection: "He conformed before the wars, but was so far from the new Conformity, as settled at the Restoration, that upon his deathbed he professed great satisfaction at his having refused it."[32]

---

25. Ann Hughes, *Politics, Society and Civil War in Warwickshire, 1620–1660* (Cambridge: Cambridge University Press, 1987), 69.

26. Ibid., 86.

27. Douglas V. Jones, *The Royal of Town Sutton-Coldfield: A Commemorative History* ([UK] Westwood, 1984), 37.

28. Quoted in Stephen J. Casselli, "Anthony Burgess' *Vindiciae Legis* and the 'Fable of Unprofitable Scholasticism': A Case Study in the Reappraisal of Seventeenth Century Reformed Scholasticism" (PhD diss., Westminster Theological Seminary, 2007), 52.

29. Hughes, *Politics, Society and Civil War*, 64.

30. E. C. Vernon, "Anthony Burgess," *Oxford Dictionary of National Biography*, accessed at http://www.oxforddnb.com/view/article/3973?docPos=1, accessed 8/2/2011

31. Ibid.

32. Quoted in ibid. See Edmund Calamy, *The Nonconformists Memorial: Being an Account of Ministers Who Were Ejected or Silenced after the Restoration*, vol. 3 (London: W. Harris, 1775).

It was during this second pastoral charge in Sutton Coldfield, just after his years working with the Westminster Assembly, that Burgess wrote his treatises on assurance (1652 and 1654, respectively).[33] All told, he spent the better part of thirty years serving the same church, only leaving under intense persecution. During his brief stint at St. Lawrence Jewry in London, he undertook to reform the church, effectively establishing a congregational presbytery, that is, a church led by elders from within the church itself. We will misunderstand the emphasis of Burgess's writings on assurance if we forget his experiences as a pastor.

Scholar

Next we must look at Burgess's formative educational context. Here we must heavily rely on what we know in general about the kind of education that Burgess received. We know something of the schools he attended and of the type of study that would have been required of him.

It is important to remind ourselves at this point that Burgess's writings on assurance did not arise from nowhere. They were the product of a mind shaped extensively by the education he had received as a young man, both in grammar school and then later during his years at Cambridge University. To understand Burgess and the particular role he played in expanding on the consensus reached by the Westminster Assembly on the matter of assurance, we must understand the education he received and the particular habits of thought that such an education would have inculcated in

33. It should be noted that Burgess's work on assurance was his first major work following the Westminster Assembly. This notwithstanding the fact that Richard Baxter's *Aphorimes on Justification* was published in 1649. Burgess would later forcefully respond to this book of Baxter's, and we know that Burgess was aware of it, since it was dedicated to him, Burgess and Baxter having spent time together in Coventry.

him. It is my contention that Burgess's work on assurance was quite closely related to his formative educational experience; he wrote and reasoned in much the same way as he had been taught—though not perhaps always arriving at the same conclusions as would have been prevalent or popular during his days as a student at Cambridge.

What is important to establish beyond question, however, is the method in which he had been trained. To establish this, we will have to go into some detail about the education that Burgess received. This will in turn show the ways in which he might be expected to engage in theological discourse, especially, in this case, when addressing matters of assurance and saving faith. What we will show is that the methodology he employs to such great effect in his treatises on assurance was well established in his mind long before he took up pen to write. Burgess's educational background seems to have been quite formative in this, and it is to this that we must turn.

Grammar School

First, of course, would have been Burgess's time in grammar school. This would have been rigorous by modern standards, especially in its emphasis on classical literature. Casselli, quoting from Foster, has compiled a partial list of works with which Burgess must have been familiar before the age of twelve or thirteen. These include "Livy, Terence, Isocrates, Justin, Caesar, Erasmus, Virgil, Epictetus, Plutarch, Ovid, Tully, Hesiod, Homer, Pindar, Xenophon, Sophocles, Euripides, Aristophanes, Horace, Seneca, and Quintilian."[34] This surely explains Burgess's prolific use of classical quotations in his own sermons and treatises. These were sources ingrained in Burgess's mind from his earliest education.

---

34. Casselli, "Anthony Burgess' *Vindiciae Legis*," 31–32.

Another point worth noting about this formative grammar school experience is the extent to which it was intended to prepare the mind for deep study. Richard Muller connects curriculum with theology, or at least with theological method, when he writes, "The educational patterns alone stand as a fundamental source of the orthodoxy, particularly in its nominally scholastic forms."[35] For Burgess, the depths required by even these early years would set the stage for what was to come.

As Watson notes, the schools of Burgess's day, in contrast with the schools of the medieval period in England, emphasized Latin grammar and rhetoric, rather than the formalities of logic.[36] Watson goes so far as to characterize the medieval schools this way: "Thus it would be, on the whole, more in accordance with facts to call the medieval schools 'logic-schools' rather than 'grammar schools.'"[37] The Latin they taught was not generally from the highest and best sources of literary Latin, but this had changed by the time of Burgess. The shift in focus, already entrenched by the time of Burgess's grammar school education, meant that the earliest years of education were spent primarily learning Latin through the reading and emulation of classical literature. One example, taken from a proposed curriculum in 1528, suggests eight classes:

> Class i—to contain less forward boys, who were to be diligently exercised in the eight parts of speech, 'whose flexible accent it should be your chief concern to form, making them respect the elements assigned them, *with the most distinct and exact pronunciation.*'

> Class ii—to practice Latin-speaking. New phrases to be written down in note-books. Lily's *Carmen Moitorium*, or Cato's *Precepts* to be studied with a view of *forming the accent.*

---

35. Muller, *Post-Reformation Reformed Dogmatics*, 1:42.
36. Foster Watson, *The Old Grammar Schools* (Cambridge: Cambridge University Press, 1916), 3.
37. Ibid., 7.

Class iii—to read authors of a familiar style, 'Who more humorous than Aesop? Who more useful than Terence?'

Class iv—'When you exercise the soldiership of the fourth class, what general would you rather have than Virgil himself, the prince of all poets? Whose majesty of verse, it were worth while should be pronounced with due intonation of voice.'

Class v—Some select epistles of Cicero.

Class vi—History—that of Sallust or of Julius Caesar . . .

Class vii—Horace's *Epistle's* of Ovid's *Metamorphoses* or *Fasti*, with occasional efforts by the pupils themselves at versification or epistle writing. Latin verse to be turned into Latin prose, and *vice versa*. Learning by heart, for which the best time is just before retiring to rest.

Class viii—The higher precepts of grammar to be taught.[38]

Although Burgess entered grammar school sometime after this list was published, it does not seem as if the basic curriculum was much changed.[39] As this example makes clear, the grammar schools of Burgess's day were aptly named. Their emphasis was on learning the language of Latin, and even the areas of study that seemed to stray beyond this were handled within the Latin curriculum. It must be noted at this point that we cannot say with absolute certainty whether Burgess's grammar school followed the precise form described by Wolsey, set out, as it was, in the century before Burgess's study. However, it can be said that, in terms of its basic framework and priorities, Burgess's grammar school would likely have followed this basic pattern.

Therefore, it should come as no surprise, when one reads Burgess, to find that he makes frequent references to classical Latin sources.

---

38. From a written address to the Masters of Ipswich School by Wolsey on September 1, 1528. Quoted in ibi.d, 17–18.
39. Watson, *Old Grammar Schools*, 78.

These were the primary sources Burgess studied from the age of six or seven.[40] And it should also come as no surprise that Burgess's later theological work, particularly his work on assurance, was exceptionally thorough. Again we note Muller's observation about depth of education leading to depth of theological interaction. Casselli gives a partial list of classical authors he would have had to have studied by the age of twelve or thirteen.

Also relevant to Burgess's later development as a pastor and theological writer was his early study of the Bible and of biblical languages. These early forays into the teaching of biblical languages began to intensify at times when the contrast between Roman Catholic and Protestant churches became starker. According to Watson, the degree to which the controversy with Roman Catholicism developed was directly related to the degree to which grammar schools began teaching the boys Greek and often even Hebrew. Controversy "led to the manifest requirement of the study of 'holy' languages, Greek, Hebrew, and Latin, associated with the earliest manuscripts of the Bible."[41] It seems likely that Burgess, obviously well trained in Latin from an early age, may also have had an early start on Greek; possibly he possessed some familiarity with the Hebrew language as well. At any rate, whether or not he learned these languages in grammar school, he did seem to show an understanding of both languages by the time of his writings on assurance.

In addition, logic and rhetoric—which, as we will see, made up the better part of his university studies—were introduced as early as grammar school. Though formal logic did not constitute the greatest

---

40. Watson writes, "The entrance age was usually seven years, though sometimes six and sometimes eight was prescribed." Watson, *Old Grammar Schools*, 116.
41. Watson, *Old Grammar Schools*, 96.

part of his early training (Latin did), it was probably introduced in some measure, even at this early stage.

Finally, the grammar school of Burgess's day would have used a catechism, probably either Nowell's (published in 1570) or Calvin's.[42] Attendance at Sunday and holy-day services was required of all, and typically schoolmasters would examine their pupils on Mondays regarding the content of the Sunday sermon.[43] In reality, the line between forming piety and developing the skills of logic and rhetoric is hard to draw. It appears that the examinations on theological matters were designed to form the students' ability in logic and rhetoric; as well, nearly all the rhetorical and logical exercises in the grammar school were related to religious and theological themes.[44]

The University Curriculum

Many of these same emphases would continue into the university years. Burgess earned his bachelor of arts degree at Cambridge University, having studied at St. John's College. Because of the particular rigor of the grammar school curriculum at the time, students matriculating at the colleges within Cambridge and Oxford Universities would have been expected to have competency in the classical trivium. In addition to this competency (which would have included a fluency in Latin), students at St. John's College from 1524 onward were expected to gain a working knowledge of Greek and Hebrew in their studies, though whether they would have gained this formally in their grammar school might have varied from individual

---

42. Ibid., 90.
43. Ibid., 91.
44. Ibid., 91.

to individual.[45] Certainly with Burgess, his knowledge of each of Greek, Hebrew, and Latin was employed extensively in his writings.

At its core, the scholastic curriculum of the seventeenth century strove toward producing able disputants. Costello, in writing about the aim of the training regimen at Cambridge during Burgess's years there, writes this:

> The typical scholastic was not likely to be a sensitive thinker, pouring out his thoughts onto pages for others to read or not as they chose. He was rather a proselytizer for his own opinions, eager 'to divide truth from error,' to best his adversary here and now, to secure acceptance of his ideas by disciples and contemporaries. He had a passion for enunciation, was forever expounding, defining, distinguishing, and disputing. The scholastics were before all else teachers, and their philosophy was intended to live, not in the library, but in the hurly-burly of the schools.[46]

The courses of study were designed to prepare students for making well-reasoned, persuasive arguments. The use of syllogisms in particular was vital in the formation of these arguments. This, as we will see, plays a key role in Burgess's discussions on assurance: he seems to closely follow the patterns of argumentation that were formed in students at Cambridge during his time of training.

Costello, in his analysis of the seventeenth-century Scholastic curriculum, identifies three key characteristics in the type of university education Burgess would have received in his Cambridge days. First, he contends that it was dialectical in nature.[47] By this, he means that it tended toward emphasizing formal logic and disputation.[48] While this would manifest itself in the essays that

45. James Kelsey McConica, *English Humanists and Reformation Politics under Henry VIII and Edward VI* (Oxford: Clarendon, 1965), 79.
46. William T. Costello, *The Scholastic Curriculum at Early Seventeenth-Century Cambridge* (Cambridge, MA: Harvard University Press, 1958), 8–9.
47. Ibid., 8.
48. Ibid.

undergraduates would be assigned, it was also seen—perhaps most clearly—in the actual verbal disputations in which they would engage. Much of Burgess's course of study would have consisted of verbal disputations on philosophical matters. The Cambridge colleges in the early seventeenth century placed a particularly high value on verbal disputation. In fact, this methodological distinctive of the seventeenth-century Cambridge education was perhaps unprecedented. Costello has suggested that this was indeed a distinctive approach to education practiced during many centuries at Cambridge, writing, "No system of thought had held its patent of monopoly for so long."[49] This "system of [educational] thought" extended not only to the disputations, for which it is justly famous, but also to the undergraduate lectures themselves.

The second of Costello's three characteristics is the emphasis on Aristotle and Aristotelian philosophy.[50] As many have noted, Aristotle's thought loomed large over the education one received in the school. However, it should be noted that, in his writings on assurance, Burgess does not appeal to Aristotle at any significant points, and he never cites Aristotle as a final authority in his polemical treatises or sermons. In fact, while it is probably undeniable that Burgess imbibed a great deal of methodological input from his study of Aristotle, it does not appear that he saw Aristotle's *conclusions* to be of any particular theological significance. In short, this part of the scholastic education is best seen in Burgess's method of arguing, rather than his conclusions.[51]

The third trait that Costello identifies is systemization.[52] What Costello means by this is that the early-seventeenth-century educational environment in which Burgess was trained undertook to

49. Ibid., 9.
50. Ibid.
51. See especially chapter 5 of this book.
52. Costello, *Scholastic Curriculum*, 10.

connect all aspects of learning into a coherent and connected whole. Individual topics were not to be considered piecemeal; they were parts of a greater framework. Broadly speaking, this kind of grand philosophical systemization was not Burgess's life's work, but at a narrower level, Burgess does evince these systematizing traits within the framework of his theology. That is, although he does quite clearly mine the entirety of his systematic theology to address whatever isolated questions of doctrine or practice he is concerned with, this again is not systematizing on the order of what Costello describes. It might reasonably be said to have come from the same habits of mind that his undergraduate curriculum sought to develop.

The University Exercises

Having looked at the broad characteristics of Burgess's undergraduate education, it is now worthwhile to examine some of the specific features that made up that broader picture. Especially given the relevance of the syllogism for Burgess's later work, it is perhaps appropriate to consider the typical exercises employed in the training of a Cambridge undergraduate in the years of Burgess's education at St. John's. These, as much as the curriculum, may have contributed to his method of theological reasoning.

The first external form employed was the lecture. To varying degrees, depending on the lecturer, this was highly systematized, with larger concepts being subdivided into questions and articles.[53] These lectures were often given daily. Although Casselli correctly asserts that the lecture typically began with a question, it is also worth noting that, prior to the lecture proper, the lecturer would often start by reviewing the previous day's lesson.[54] This is noteworthy because

53. Ibid., 14.
54. Casselli, "Anthony Burgess' *Vindicaiae Legis*," 37.

many of Burgess's own sermons are structured in the same fashion: review of previous addresses, followed by an opening question or assertion, which is then examined more closely.[55] In any event, a formal logical case (perhaps preceded by review) made up the form of the lecture. And while there were differences of opinion on certain aspects of this form early on (such as whether or not students should take or copy written notes), the basic format was well established and practiced by the time of Burgess's arrival at Cambridge.[56] In fact, the question of writing notes was well settled by Burgess's time: students were expected to write the lecture nearly completely while listening.[57] It is certainly possible—one might even think it likely—that this affected Burgess's own thinking as he developed arguments, either in writing or orally, though he does not explicitly refer to these experiences in his later career.[58]

Of perhaps more significance than the exercise of the lecture were those of the disputation and declamation, which together with the lecture formed the three major exercises of early-seventeenth-century Cambridge undergraduate studies.[59] In fact, even in Burgess's own day, the disputation, rather than the lecture, was considered to be the core element of the curriculum. Costello describes it this way: "Within the colleges, disputations were held frequently and informally (*sine ulla praefationea*). At Trinity College, for example,

---

55. See, for instance, his method of argumentation in the beginning of Anthony Burgess, *Spiritual Refining: Or a Treatise of Grace and Assurance* (London: Thomas Underhill, 1652).
56. Costello, *Scholastic Curriculum*, 10–11.
57. Ibid., 15.
58. This basic idea is in line with what many have said about scholasticism in the seventeenth century, showing its bearing on *method* rather than *content*. See, for instance, Richard A. Muller, *Dictionary of Latin and Greek Theological Terms: Drawn Principally from Protestant Scholastic Theology* (Grand Rapids: Baker, 1985), 8. See also John A. Trentman, "Scholasticism in the Seventeenth Century," in *The Cambridge History of Later Medieval Philosophy: From the Rediscovery of Aristotle to the Disintegration of Scholasticism 100–1600*, ed. Norman Kretzman, Anthony Kenney, and Jan Pinborg (Cambridge: Cambridge University Press, 1982), 818–37.
59. Casselli, "Anthony Burgess' *Vindiciae Legis*," 37.

disputations were held thrice weekly in chapel, on Monday, Wednesday, and Friday, either in Philosophy or Theology. Sophisters (those who had not reached bachelorhood) disputed on rhetoric, dialectics, and the problems of Aristotle."[60]

It is also worth quoting Costello's summation of the primary tool in engaging in an effective disputation—namely, the syllogism:

> In every case, the opponent follows a carefully plotted line of syllogisms designed to trap the answerer into a position where he may be logically forced, step by step, into admitting the exact opposite of his thesis. *The syllogistic presentation is mandatory,* as James Duport says in his rules for students: 'Dispute always Syllogistically, at *least* Enthmematically and as much as you can Categorically.' But, the syllogistic attack was not to produce a cut-and-dried crop of logical forms. 'When you dispute,' admonishes Duport, 'be sure you gett the Arguments perfectly by heart, & take heede of that dull, cold, idle, way of reading Syllogismes out of a paper, for so one can never dispute with life and courage.'[61]

The key here, of course, is the importance of developing the syllogism and the "syllogistic presentation" when arguing a disputed point. The student in Burgess's setting would have had to identify no fewer than forty-five illegitimate syllogistic forms and be able to answer and point out any one of the thirteen classical fallacies.[62]

Finally, students had to engage in declamation. Costello defines this as "a set speech, designed to show rhetorical and literary proficiency. It varied in length from two hundred words to several thousand, and might be on any subject from the meretriciousness of Penelope to the rumoured suspension of Mohammed's corpse between two magnets."[63] Surely this too had an effect on Burgess's later writing and preaching ministry. In fact, the *clerum,* a subset of

60. Costello, *Scholastic Curriculum*, 14.
61. Ibid., 20 (italics mine).
62. Casselli, "Anthony Burgess' *Vindiciae Legis*," 39.
63. Costello, *Scholastic Curriculum*, 32.

the declamation, was also a part of the curriculum. It was a formal sermon, preached occasionally to clergy who were present for the occasion.[64]

Casselli characterizes each of the three exercises—lecture, disputation, and declamation—noting, "All of these exercises required the rigorous application of logic and rhetoric to particular problems or questions."[65] And as we have noted, the syllogism and the syllogistic form or reasoning formed the essence of this application of logic. In a sense, one can observe Burgess arguing along the lines of this form in all his writings. More specifically, a syllogistic framework characterizes his basic understanding of certain important elements of pastoral theology, most notably (as has already been mentioned) his doctrine of assurance.

Anthony Burgess was eminent in his studies at Cambridge, where after his education at St. John's, he served as a tutor at Emmanuel College. Perhaps as a fitting summary of his undergraduate education, we should note that Burgess's academic prowess is noted in the *History of the University of Cambridge* this way: "Among the *learned* writers of this College [St. John's], I have omitted many still alive, as Mr. *Anthony* Burgess."[66]

Graduate Studies

Anthony Burgess was not only a product of his grammar school and undergraduate education, as formative as those periods of training would prove to be; he also earned a master of arts degree at Cambridge. Since we will argue that his educational background

---

64. Ibid., 33.
65. Casselli, "Anthony Burgess' *Vindiciae Legis*," 37.
66. Thomas Fuller, *The History of the University of Cambridge: And of Waltham Abbey with the Appeal of Injured Innocence* (London: Thomas Tegg, 1840), 207.

helps us understand his contribution to the Reformed doctrine of assurance, it is worth understanding just what this graduate course of study would have entailed for Burgess, and what his particular focus on theological studies would have meant in the era of which he was a part.

First, it must be understood that in seventeenth-century universities in general, and in Cambridge in particular, theology held sway. The study of divinity was considered to be the most important of the academic fields, and the one most worthy of study beyond the undergraduate days. In a history of the founding of Harvard College (in 1642, by men educated at Cambridge), one figure is quoted as saying, "All but Divinity had very little importance in our period. There were no proper facilities for the study of 'physic' at Cambridge or Oxford. . . . The reformation made the civil and canon historical studies of no direct professional value; the common lawyers had what amounted to a law school of their own at the Inns of Court. The music degrees, toward which no instruction was provided, were little regarded and seldom taken."[67] Costello writes emphatically, "No historian of the seventeenth century can afford to ignore the paramountcy of theology in university life, much less dare he minimize the issues."[68] Theology, often called the queen of the sciences, was king of the Cambridge curriculum.

Aside from clear understanding of the primacy of theology in the graduate studies at the Cambridge colleges of the seventeenth century, it is also once again important to grasp the methods employed by those undertaking this course of study. What we find is that, like the undergraduate curriculum at Cambridge, the graduate course of study likewise revolved around disputations. For at least

---

67. Quoted in Samuel Eliot Morison, *The Founding of Harvard College* (Cambridge: Fellows of Harvard College, 1935; repr. 1995), 60 n. 1.
68. Costello, *Scholastic Curriculum*, 107.

some of the colleges of that era, these disputations on divinity were held on a weekly basis.[69] Costello rightly refers to these disputations in theology as "the acme of the school exercises."[70] These disputations were not dissimilar to what Burgess would have heard and participated in during his time as an undergraduate. Certainly, we will see that the kind of theological precision and skill in argumentation required by this kind of exercise is characteristic of Burgess's writing on assurance.

The normal day for a graduate student at a Cambridge college during that period would begin at five with morning chapel. Two or three times a week, this chapel service would be followed by a ten- or fifteen-minute sermon delivered by either BD or MA students. From the time of breakfast at six till lunch at eleven, there were lectures and time for study. From one in the afternoon onward, students were expected to study in their rooms or attend one of the aforementioned public disputations. Then there would be a break at four, supper at six, and generally speaking, a meeting for an hour or two with the tutor before going to bed.[71]

As for what the graduate student in divinity might read, we can turn to a manuscript found in the St. John's College library. In it, an older theologian advises a student of divinity on what books he should read, and then on how he should prepare his sermons:

> When ye are ripe of understanding, to reade them with some judgement, some Schoolmen will bee usefull; read first Lombard, then Aquinas, then Estius, Ferrariensis, or Caietan, or Bannes, or some others of his followers, then Scotus (most iudicious as well as subtile) & some of his followers, especially Lichettus & Rhada, also Sancta Clara, Deus, Natura & Gratia & those yt gather his philosophy, as Faber Faventinus on his Physicke, Merisse on his Metaphysicks . . . Bronius his Annals,

69. *Documents Relating to the University and Colleges of Cambridge* (London, 1852), 3:505, 3:558.
70. Costello, *Scholastic Curriculum*, 112.
71. Morison, *Founding*, 63–64.

who hath made a long & learned Collection of Ecclesiastical story, & digested it into a good method, & will be much advantage for a full comprehension of Ecclesiastical Storie; But take heed how Yu trust him, for 1. He makes use of many spurious Authors 2. Hee endeavors reight or wrong, to advance the Papall Monarchy, & to this, makes great flourishes with false Authors & misquotes, & misconstrues those that are true.[72]

This goes on, finally closing with these words for the theological student: "Soe much in Answere to yr Importunate desires, though yu might have consulted many fitter in such Businesse; for as I have not had ye opportunitie to search many vast Libraries, yet I durst not commend unto yu those that I have not tried, but reseaved only by report of others (save some very fewe) & therefore am faine to fetch almost all ye materials out of the compasse of mine owne private studye."[73]

Finally, he closes with these words on preaching: "Fetch ye matter of yr sermons, not only from yr Bookes, & Invention, but from ye Consideration 1) of yr own experience, 2) or yr peoples necessityes, sinnes & miseryes."[74] We have no evidence that Burgess himself was aware of this exact device, nor do we know if he read and absorbed all the books recommended for this divinity graduate student (these are only excerpts from the manuscript), but we can say with certainty that his exposure was fairly deep, even if he was only a typical Cambridge divinity student. And we will certainly see that, whoever the mentor and student happen to be in the manuscript just quoted from, the advice of the older man to his questioner about the sources of preaching were most certainly heeded.

We can also say that Burgess's time as a graduate student was a success from the standpoint of Emmanuel College. Just before he

72. MS. K 38, St John's Library, Cambridge.
73. Ibid.
74. Ibid.

completed his master's degree there in 1630, he was invited to serve as a fellow at Emmanuel College.[75] This position he held for five years, and it was as a result of his work during this time that we receive one of our few quotes directly addressing Burgess's academic achievement. The quote is from one of his students, John Wallis. Wallis was to be a secretary of the Westminster Assembly and later served as Savillian Professor of Mathematics at Oxford in 1649. Wallis wrote of his time in Cambridge, "About Christmas 1632, I was sent to the University of Cambridge, and there admitted in Immanuel-College, under the tuition of Mr. Anthony Burgess, a pious, learned, and able scholar, a good disputant, and a good tutor."[76]

We must understand that tutors had a great deal of control over their students. Morison gives this picture of the relationship between the tutor and the student in the seventeenth century at Cambridge:

> A college tutor at that time had almost absolute control over his pupils, with whom his relation was more than paternal. He seldom had more than six pupils, and usually less; for he was supposed to spend much time on his own studies. He might be highly conscientious, or otherwise, 'Most tutors I have known,' wrote a Cambridge graduate in 1646, 'if they read twice a day and took account of that, held themselves sufficiently discharged of their trust; few did so much.' He might teach his pupils in a class, or individually. But, in any case, one or more pupils shared his chamber, his compensation was a matter of personal arrangement with their parents, and he was responsible to the college for all their bills.[77]

Burgess's role as a tutor ended after five years, but it is difficult to argue with the notion that he imbibed the essence of what it meant to

75. Oxford Dictionary of National Biogrphy, s.v. "Burgess, Anthony." Accessed online on 3/1/15 http://www.oxforddnb.com/view/article/3973?docPos=1
76. John Wallis, quoted in James Reid, *Memoirs and Lives and Writings of those Eminent Divines, who Convened in the Famous Assembly at Westminster, in the Seventeenth Century* (Paisley: Stephen and Andrew Young, 1811), 146.
77. Morison, *Founding*, 62–63.

be educated at Cambridge University during his time there.[78] He was prepared for his work as an undergraduate, was successful enough to enter Emmanuel immediately for a master's degree, and afterward was asked to serve as a fellow—a position at which he seems to have had great success.

In short, up to and through the 1640s, students at Cambridge followed a path of learning defined by the scholastic method. It appears that the distinctive lecture format was in place nearly until the end of the 1600s; the disputation lasted until the 1640s, and the writing of declamations—with an ear tuned to how they would sound when read aloud—continued along with it.[79] Scholasticism, with its logical rigor and attention to oral examination and disputes, was alive and well at the Cambridge of which Burgess was a part. It is perhaps no surprise that he took that training and used it to fill in the gaps left in the Westminster Assembly's discussion of assurance.

It is also worth pointing out again the depth of reading and interaction that Burgess likely engaged in as part of his formative education. We must understand that he and those educated in a similar style and context were widely read in a variety of sources. As some of the apparently typical reading lists indicate, the men studying at Burgess's colleges did not limit themselves to one particular era of authors, nor to one specific viewpoint. The education was catholic in the sense of its breadth and scope. Perry Miller is worth quoting at length on this general point:

---

78. The statutes of Emmanuel College made each fellowship only temporary, with the aim of pushing men into church work and not academic careers. In 1627, the fellows asked Charles I to suspend this rule, which he did; however, Anthony Burgess, along with five others, petitioned against this suspension. Apparently they felt that the needs in the church were still too great to allow Emmanuel fellows to pursue exclusively academic careers. This would seem to underscore the earlier points made in this chapter about Burgess's essentially pastoral orientation, even in the midst of his strong academic record. For more on this incident, see Sarah Bendall et al., *A History of Emmanuel College, Cambridge* (Rochester, NY: Boydell, 1999), 24–28; see also Casselli, "Anthony Burgess' *Vindiciae Legis*," 47–48.

79. Costello, *Scholastic Curriculum*, 146–47.

For the content of their belief, for the meanings which they read into Scripture or the principles they deduced from it, the Puritans both in England and New England drew freely upon the stores of knowledge and the methods of thinking which were then available to educated men. Like other persons of cultivation in the period, they profited, sometimes deliberately, sometimes unwillingly, from the advantages of their location in the intellectual history of Europe. At the commencement of the seventeenth century it seemed as though many different countries of the mind as well as of the world, many continents of thought and many trade routes of culture, lay simultaneously ready at hand for intellectual exploitation. Piety did not inhibit the Puritan scholar from adventuring upon them.[80]

Excursus on Scholasticism

One of the categories that could be used to describe the product of Burgess's education, as well as Goodwin's and Owen's, is the term *Scholasticism*. Brian Armstrong articulated with particular clarity a category that, for many, came to define the writings of the late-sixteenth- and seventeenth-century Reformed theologians.[81] Giving the label "Reformed Scholasticism" to this era, he identified its major features:

(1) Primarily it will have reference to that theological approach which asserts religious truth on the basis of deductive ratiocination from given assumptions or principles, thus producing a logically coherent and defensible system of belief. Generally this takes the form of syllogistic reasoning. It is an orientation, it seems, invariably based upon an

---

80. Perry Miller, *The New England Mind in the Seventeenth Century* (Cambridge, MA: Harvard University Press, 1939), 81. For another helpful view of the "catholicity" of learning that John Owen received at Oxford during this time, see Carl R. Trueman, *John Owen: Reformed Catholic, Renaissance Man* (Hampshire, UK: Ashgate, 2007), 7–23.

81. For conclusive evidence on the ways in which Armstrong was articulating the conclusions of many, see the survey in Richard A. Muller, "Calvin and the 'Calvinists': Assessing Continuities and Discontinuities between the Reformation and Orthodoxy," *Calvin Theological Journal* 30 (1995): 345–75.

Aristotelian philosophical commitment and so relates to medieval scholasticism. (2) The term will refer to the employment of reason in religious matters, so that reason assumes at least equal standing with faith in theology, thus jettisoning some of the authority of revelation. (3) It will comprehend the sentiment that the scriptural record contains a unified, rationally comprehensible account and thus may be formed into a definitive statement which may be used as a measuring stick to determine one's orthodoxy. (4) It will comprehend a pronounced interest in metaphysical matters, in abstract, speculative thought, particularly with reference to the knowledge of God. The distinctive scholastic Protestant position is made to rest on a speculative formulation of the will of God.[82]

These characteristics were seen, by Armstrong and others, as a move away from a biblical and pastoral focus. Brian Armstrong, for instance, writes, "This new outlook represents a profound divergence from the humanistically oriented religion of John Calvin and most of the early reformers. The strong biblically and experimentally based theology of Calvin and Luther had, it is fair to say, been overcome by the metaphysics and deductive logic of a restored Aristotelianism."[83] Basil Hall writes, "The biblical exegesis became subordinated to a restored Aristotelianism, for Protestantism was recoiling before the victories of the Counter Reformation, and it was beginning to use the weapons of its adversary. . . . The polemic period of Protestant scholasticism now appearing showed less interest in both the classical humanism and the biblical humanism of the earlier period."[84]

Some, such as James B. Torrance, located the problem earlier, in the theology of Theodore Beza. Torrance writes, "The pattern [of the WCF] is no longer the Trinitarian one of the Creeds or Calvin's

---

82. Brian Armstrong, *Calvinism and the Amyraut Heresy: Protestant Scholasticism and Humanism in Seventeenth-Century France* (Madison: University of Wisconsin Press, 1969), 32.
83. Ibid., 32.
84. Basil Hall, "Calvin against the Calvinists," in *John Calvin: A Collection of Distinguished Essays*, ed. Gervase Duffield (Grand Rapids: Eerdmans, 1966), 25–26.

Institutio of 1559, but is dominated by the eternal Decrees and the scheme of Federal Theology. . . . Thus the doctrine of the decrees of God in the tradition of Theodore Beza and William Perkins becomes the major premise of the whole scheme of creation and redemption."[85]

John Stanley Bray goes further. He writes that seventeenth-century Scholasticism is "an approach to religious truth which stresses the need to discover basic assumptions or principles on which one may build a logical system of belief that would be capable of rational defense."[86] With respect to the distinction between this approach and an earlier one, he writes, "By the seventeenth century the orthodox theologians within the Reformed camp were so committed to scholasticism that they made virtually no references to Calvin, and it appears that the thought of Calvin lacked normative value for them."[87] He also writes, "The key to understanding Calvin's theology is to view him as one who desired to be a theologian of the Word; his concern was with Scripture, rather than with dogmatics. For this reason Calvin refused to distort and to twist the obvious meaning of Scripture in order to harmonize it or bring it in accord with reason."[88] Bray's implication about later Reformed writers is perfectly clear.

A better definition of Scholasticism, and one that is much more in keeping with what we observe in the work of Burgess, Goodwin, and Owen, has been proposed by Richard A. Muller:

> It is a theology designed to develop a system on a highly technical level and in an extremely precise manner by means of the careful identification of topics, division of these topics into their basic parts,

85. James B. Torrance, "Strengths and Weaknesses of the Westminster Theology," in *The Westminster Confession in the Church Today: Papers Prepared for the Church of Scotland Panel on Doctrine*, ed. Alasdair I. C. Heron (Edinburgh: St. Andrews Press, 1982), 45–46.

86. John Stanley Bray, "Theodore Beza's Doctrine of Predestination" (PhD diss., Stanford University, 1971), 6.

87. Ibid., 5.

88. Ibid., 12.

definition of the parts, and doctrinal or logical argumentation concerning the divisions and definitions. . . . The term 'scholastic' is, therefore, applicable particularly to the large-scale, systematic development of seventeenth-century Protestant theology. This approach to Protestant scholasticism, based directly on the definitions and methods evidenced in the seventeenth-century systems, explicitly opposes the view of several recent scholars according to which 'scholasticism' can be identified specifically with a use of Aristotelian philosophy, a pronounced metaphysical interest, and the use of predestination as an organizing principle in theological system. . . . Scholasticism, then, indicates the technical and logical approach to theology as a discipline characteristic of theological systems from the late twelfth through the seventeenth century.[89]

This fits with what we will see observe in the figures we are studying.[90] Although many see the Scholastic training and Scholastic methodology and presentation of the seventeenth-century English divines as leading them away from the Bible and away from the Reformers, Anthony Burgess in particular points in a different direction. While he was certainly trained in Scholastic methodology, and while his writings on assurance are often framed in syllogistic ways, his pastoral concern and biblicism cannot be overlooked.

Anthony Burgess and the Westminster Consensus

Anthony Burgess was deeply aware of the fact that the Westminster formulations needed to be expanded upon. This he did primarily in a long series of sermons, published in two volumes totaling nearly one thousand pages in length, entitled, *Spiritual Refining: Or a Treatise on Grace and Assurance*. While it is derived from sermons that were

---

89. Muller, *Post-Reformation Reformed Dogmatics,* 1:34–37.
90. In addition, as already noted, this also fits with the conclusion many others have drawn regarding the relationship between Scholasticism and the seventeenth-century English Puritans. See n. 96.

originally preached, Burgess rightly calls this work a treatise—a word that, at that time and still today, refers to "a book or writing which treats of some particular subject; commonly one containing a formal or methodical discussion or exposition of the principles of the subject."[91] This indeed describes *Spiritual Refining*. It is large-scale treatment of the topic of assurance.

This treatise on assurance has been referred to by Beeke as "an unequalled anatomy of experimental religion."[92] Whether or not this assessment is justified, it is certainly the case that Burgess's work bears a relationship to the WCF and its formulations on assurance.[93] In fact, because of Burgess's role within the Westminster Assembly, and because his treatise on assurance is at least among the most significant writings on the topic from someone who was part of the assembly, it must be viewed in terms of their relationship with the WCF.

Spiritual Refining and the WCF: Continuity and Expansion

This relationship between *Spiritual Refining* and the WCF can be seen in two ways. First, Burgess's treatise can be analyzed in terms of the extent to which it fits with the WCF formulation: Does Burgess agree with the WCF in all the important details, or does he disagree? In this case in particular, we will want to see also whether the emphases of the WCF with respect to assurance are the same as those of Burgess. Also, Burgess's writings can be analyzed in terms of how they develop themes on which the WCF is either silent or

---

91. *Oxford English Dictionary*, March 2011 online ed., "treatise," http://www.oed.com.
92. Joel Beeke, "Anthony Burgess on Assurance," in *Answer of a Good Conscience: Papers Read at the 1997 Westminster Conference*, available at http://www.westminsterconference.org.uk/pastpapers/1997, 27–52.
93. We will also have to look at Burgess's understanding of faith in order to understand his framework for assurance. Much of this is found in Anthony Burgess, *Scripture Directory for Church-Officers and People* (London: Abraham Miller, 1659).

ambiguous. That is, how do Burgess's writings fill out the WCF consensus statement on assurance?

We will see that the methodology Burgess employs in addressing the question of assurance fits with the Scholastic background described earlier and differs in focus from that of his contemporaries.[94] While there are some points of essential agreement between Burgess on the one hand and Goodwin and Owen on the other, there are also vast differences in emphasis. Although Goodwin and Owen disagree on a few points (the role of the Spirit's sealing being the primary one), their essential approach is the same. Burgess, like these two, continues with the same basic premises of the WCF, yet he expands upon its silences with a markedly different approach.

We must first look at the major ways in which Burgess affirms the Westminster consensus in his writings. To be sure, one already could make a strong case that Burgess agreed with the WCF, given his active role in its initial formulation. But as we will see, his writings only make this essential agreement clearer.

In demonstrating Burgess's agreement with the WCF statement on assurance, we will look at two questions. First, did Burgess affirm all three of the possibilities envisioned by the WCF? That is, did he see the possibility of true assurance, the possibility of false assurance, and the possibility that assurance, once gained, might be lost? The second question is this: Was Burgess clear that assurance, of the kind both he and the WCF are referring to, is of the essence of faith? These two diagnostic questions, when posed to Burgess's writings, will give us some sense of how tightly his statements can be fit together with the statements of the WCF, even as we seek to address the ways in which he goes beyond those formulations in important ways.

It can hardly be doubted that Burgess believed in the possibility of true assurance. This is the focus of his treatise, and as we will

94. See chapter 2.

see later, he gives a detailed framework for achieving it. Similarly, Burgess, perhaps more than any theologian of his era, gives the preeminent treatment of the ways in which one can receive false assurance. As we will see, because of Burgess's particular way of addressing the matter of gaining true assurance, he is required to spend a great deal of time on the problem of false assurance. So the first two possibilities envisioned by the WCF—true assurance and false assurance—are clearly envisioned by Burgess as well.

As to the third possibility envisioned by the WCF, Burgess gives at least three scriptural examples of assurance coming to a believer after some time or else coming and going. These examples are particularly instructive in that they show us that Burgess envisions the same possibilities—assurance, lack of assurance, and false assurance—that the WCF does.

To illustrate the possibility of a believer having a lack of assurance, Burgess gives the example of Mary Magdalene, whom Christ did not assure of forgiveness until she wept for her sin.[95] Another example he gives is that of the apostle Paul in Romans 7–8. Burgess interprets the Spirit of God in Romans 8 to be "*a spirit of bondage*, before it is *a spirit of adoption*."[96] Burgess adds these words to his example: "I like not the assurance that never doubted; it is like the temper of that man, who said, *all these I have kept from my youth*. It cannot be thought that so great and spiritual a mercy should be brought into your soul, and your heart not be in many commotions. Apprehensions of grace in us, accompanied with sense and feeling of our imperfections are always good symptoms, as in that man, *Lord I believe* (there was his assurance of grace in him) *help my unbelief*."[97] Burgess's other example here was David, who, Burgess says, was at times "in the dark, and

95. Burgess, *Spiritual Refining*, 19.
96. Ibid.
97. Ibid., 20.

much wavering."[98] So assurance comes and goes; indeed, mixing doubt with assurance may itself be a sign of true grace.

Yet these are not the only ways of establishing Burgess's essential agreement with the WCF framework. To look further at this relationship, we must examine Burgess's comments on the nature of true faith. While reviewing Burgess's comments on true faith in general, we will also see if assurance, of the type mentioned in the WCF, is part of its essence.

Burgess on True Faith

To begin to understand how Burgess views the doctrine of assurance, we must first examine what he says about the nature of true faith. This will give some insight into the broader questions about Burgess's concurrence with the WCF statements regarding the relationship between saving faith and assurance. It will also show us one more area in which Burgess felt it necessary to expand on the WCF statement.

Perhaps the most complete and concise description of Burgess's view of faith is found in *Spiritual Refining*, sermon XXIX.[99] In this chapter, Burgess addresses the text of James 2:26, which reads, "For as the body without the Spirit is dead, so faith without works is dead also."[100] He begins by outlining the significance of this text and its relation to the rest of the New Testament, and also summarizing the topic on which he will be writing: "James demonstrateth what kinde of Faith this is, *viz*, an actual operative one, which puts a man upon all holy duties.'[101] This "actual operative" faith stands in sharp contrast

98. Ibid.
99. Ibid., 167–73.
100. Quoted from ibid., 167.
101. Ibid.

118

to other possibilities Burgess envisions, each of which amounts to no faith at all in his estimation.

The first of these contrasting possibilities is an improper presumption. Burgess describes some who may have a "vain confidence" regarding the truth of their faith. Their so-called faith is really nothing more than presumption. The telling mark of such presumptuous faith is that it lacks "effectual operations in the way of grace." Or, to put it differently, it does not showcase the works that saving faith must necessarily bear. In such a case, Burgess says, "the Devils go further than such loose Christianity."[102]

In providing this description of what faith is not (and what presumption is), Burgess gives us a hint of his definition of real, saving faith. Saving faith, for Burgess, must of course have orthodox content. But assenting to orthodox content alone is not enough. In fact, Burgess argues that faith must have three elements: "Knowledge, Assent, and fiducial Application."[103] Though Scripture may speak of only one of these aspects at a given time, all are actually present in the biblical account—the presence of one, Burgess argues, being merely a stand-in for the presence of all three.

True faith must go far beyond a confidence in the historicity of the biblical accounts. While it begins with confidence in their truthfulness, it must move to embrace those truths as personally good. This embrace of the personal goodness of the truths will necessarily lead to acting upon and confessing those truths in life.[104] In a sense, what Burgess is arguing is that if one really believes in the great truths about Christ, this leads to further action. The theological truths themselves are so powerful that, if really understood and embraced as good, they cannot help but lead to more substantive and obvious

---

102. Ibid., 168.
103. Ibid., 169.
104. Burgess, *Scripture Directory*, 71.

fruit in the life of the believer. Here we see an important distinction for him: it is not that the works themselves are part of the faith, but rather that the substance of the faith is so personally powerful that it cannot help but lead to works. Absent those works, one must question whether there is a true understanding of the substance of the orthodox content, or a true embrace of the orthodox teaching about Christ as personally good.

It should also be noted that, for Burgess, there is not only the possibility of vain presumption (shown through a lack of works, among other things), which is no faith at all, but also the possibility of a temporary faith. Burgess does not elaborate on this phenomenon; he merely introduces it. But in his passing reference, he distinguishes it from the "miraculous faith" that is true and that leads to life.[105]

In expounding the nature of faith, and even in expanding upon it to discuss presumption and temporary faith, Burgess is quick to say that he is not attempting to be creative. He points out that his definition of faith is based on commonly accepted definitions.[106] Further, his definition is set under the broader heading of the ministry of the word. It was the word that produced faith, and it is in order to understand the ministry of the word that Burgess expounds the essence of what the Scriptures themselves produce.

The first element present in faith is "knowledge and understanding."[107] Here Burgess is mainly trying to counteract the notion that faith is blind. He employs the example of the incarnation of Christ and the Trinity. Although it is true that no one can fully understand either of these doctrines in a way that reconciles their apparent inherent contradictions, Burgess argues that one can still embrace them in an understanding way by having confident

---

105. Ibid., 69.
106. Ibid., 71.
107. Ibid.

knowledge in the ground of these doctrines, namely, the Scriptures themselves. He puts it this way: "To say a blind faith, is as great a contradiction, as to say, a dark Sunne, or a cold fire. If it be faith, it doth see the ground of its belief. Indeed, faith cannot comprehend the matter we believe, the Doctrine of the Trinity, the Incarnation of Christ, are like the dazelling Sunne to our Bats-eye; but though faith cannot comprehend the matter believed, *yet it knoweth the ground why it doth believe*, in those places of Scripture, and the testimony of Gods Word."[108]

Burgess, following the well-worn paths which he readily acknowledged, also includes assent in his definition of faith. To know something might imply only understanding a fact but not recognizing it to be true. His primary proof of this is Heb. 11:1. From this passage, which talks about faith consisting of the "substance of things not seen," Burgess concludes that "substance" implies making something real, acting as if it were entirely true. He writes, "*Faith is the substance*, Heb 11.1. that is, by faith we make those things that are future really subsist, as it were in our souls, as if present: Thus Faith makes Heaven and Hell present. The Apostolic excellently describes it, *They behold not the things temporal, or seen, but the things eternal which are not seen*."[109] Seeing what is unseen involves a mental assent, living in light of what one knows for certain to be true.

For his third characteristic of faith, Burgess turns from the general to the specific. His description of the third aspect applies directly to saving faith and not more generally to all aspects of beliefs that Christians hold. It is called by Burgess "*That which is the compleat and formal act of faith*."[110] It is resting in, receiving, or coming to Christ. For Burgess, this is intimately tied to union with Christ.

108. Ibid.
109. Ibid.
110. Ibid.

It is powerful because of the "ligaments" that it ties to Christ. It has strength because it involves "Christ dwelling in our hearts." It is the "marrow, and the soul of faith, when a man *so knoweth, so assents,* as thereby he is *incorporated* into Christ, *recieivng of his virtue and influence.*"[111] This, according to Burgess, is what separates true believers from false. While false believers may have an understanding, and even a confidence in things spoken of in the Scriptures, this understanding is not efficacious or powerful, since they have not been united to Christ through it.

Elsewhere he uses the analogy of saving faith being like a marriage:

> Thus *John Baptist* calls himself *the friend of the Bridegroom*, John 3.29 which is the duty of every Minister; the friend of the Bridegroom, which standeth and heareth, rejoiceth greatly because of the Bridegrooms voice. It's an allusion to the custome in those dayes; the Bridegroom he had his friend and spokesman to bring him into the Brides presence, and he heard their conference; if there were a willing agreement between them concluded, then the friend rejoiced greatly. Thus it was with *John,* and also with every Minister: We are Christs spokesman, we wooe you, we entreat you, we bring you and Christ together every Sabbath day. Bow if any soul will receive him, and be married to him, forsaking his former lusts, and all by-past sinnes, then is the friend of the Bridegrooms joy greatly fulfilled; it would therefore be horrible unfaithfulness in us, if we should do as *Sampson's* friend did to him, who got *Sampson's* wife for himself.[112]

For Burgess, the language of spiritual union is used to illustrate the bond between Christ and the believer. This spiritual union is effected through the preaching of God's word. Burgess writes that the preaching of the word is *the* ordinary and necessary means by which God works in the hearts and consciences of people:

> *The Ministry is the only ordinary way* that God hath appointed, either for

111. Ibid.
112. Ibid., 63.

the beginnings or increase of grace. For the beginnings, Thus *Faith* is said *to come by hearing*, Rom 10:17. *And God hath begotten by his Word*, Jam. 1.18. And for the increase, *Eph.* 4. You may there see it is for the compleating of us in *a full stature of Christ*. Thus as the ordinary way of a mans life is by outward food and sustenance; so the ordinary meanes of all spiritual life is by the Ministry of the Word. Indeed some propound particular cases, as of Infants who do not hear, or of deaf men, or of some persons by unexpected calamities [illegible, possibly 'can'] where no Ministry is to be had; but we do not now speak of extraordinary wayes, we know God did feed the *Israelites* with *Manna* from heaven when they could have no ordinary food; but in Gods ordinary way, unless thou expect a miracle, the Ministry is the instrumental publique means.[113]

Burgess's two emphases—the necessity of the word of God as the basis for understanding faith, and the reality of faith *always* manifesting itself in good works—serve to lay the groundwork for Burgess's entire superstructure of the doctrine of assurance.

The Effects of Faith

In light of Burgess's third element of faith—union with Christ—it comes as no surprise that the two effects of faith on which he expounds are related to what Christ gives through union with him. Because we know already that true faith will be recognizable through the fruit borne from it, we must briefly overview the effects of union with Christ, according to Burgess. The first of these is his righteousness. To Burgess, the starting point for an understanding of the value of faith is found in realizing the value of Christ's imputed righteousness. It is, in his estimation, the only proper starting point for understanding the life of faith as a whole. It is the ground for Christian obedience and for freedom from guilt. An extended

---

113. Ibid., 69.

quotation is in order, to demonstrate just how far-reaching and foundational Burgess believed imputed righteousness to be:

> This is the *hand* to put on those glorious Robes to cover our nakednesse. This is the *eye* by which we look upon that exalted Serpent to be healed. It's *not repenting, sorrowing, reforming,* no nor *martyrdom* itself, that hath this honour, which *faith* hath; neither is this for any *dignity*, or *worth* of faith, but because it's an *instrument to receive the righteousnesse of Christ*, which no other grace can be. So that as the child new born, presently moves it lips and mouth for the brest, to be sucking there: So the new born spiritual Infant immediately goeth out of its own works, it's own righteousnesse, and desireth to be found in Christ onely. This way of believing is very paradoxical, and hidden to a guilty conscience; *Cain* did not know it, *Judas* was not acquainted with it, and thereupon eternally perished.[114]

Burgess sees this justifying faith as the grounds for sanctification. He also sees justification as grounded on the notion of imputed righteousness. He considers this the first *ad intra* effect of faith. The second *ad intra* effect relates directly to sanctification.

For the believer to overcome temptation and bring forth fruit, he or she must, in Burgess's words, apply Christ in faith. It is essential, in Burgess's thinking, for the converted Christian to continually come to Christ in faith in order to be sanctified. He writes, "But oh how hard it is, ere many of the children of God come to learn this good way! They lie discouraged in their combate and conflict with sinne; they are ashamed of their hypocrisie, their guile. Oh they are so unworthy, and so wretched that they dare not come neer Christ, and this hinders them!"[115] It was essential in his thinking that Christians not be overcome with guilt and therefore turn away from the source of their sanctification. Burgess states unequivocally that the believer can *"receive virtue and power from Christ to subdue our corruptions, to*

114. Ibid, 72.
115. Ibid.

conquer our sinnes; so that faith is the instrument of Sanctification, as well as Justification."

But how is this to work? How is someone to rest in and appropriate the mercies of Christ by faith in an ongoing manner? Burgess does not state this with mechanical precision, but he does offer metaphors and examples. And as evidenced in the previous quotation, he often offers counter-examples as well.

The first image, a well-worn one given by Jesus himself, is that of branches on a vine. Here Burgess likens the ability to overcome sin as the effect of the sap coming from a vine and producing fruit: "And as these are nourished and enlivened, bringing forth fruit, by having sap and virtue from the head or tree; so are we supplied with virtue and efficacy for all imperfections by faith from Christ."[116]

The primary counterexample offered is that of Peter resisting Jesus Christ's offer of foot washing. Burgess sees this to be a perfect example of the how believers can resist the work of Christ in the midst of their weakness. Moving to another metaphor, to fail to come to Christ is to throw away a weapon in the midst of a heated battle.[117]

Burgess moves from the internal ways in which faith is essential to the external ways in which true faith will be expressed and known. First, Burgess says that someone possessing true faith will cleanse himself from filthiness both outwardly and inwardly. He assumes that many will profess to know Christ, to be joined with him through faith. But if such a profession is not joined by some kind of cleansing, it cannot be genuine. For Burgess, this is implied in the notion that to have true faith is to be joined with Christ. Joining with Christ—having Christ dwell in one's heart—will necessarily lead to an incompatibility with whatever wickedness or impurity is there. Burgess states the implication of this succinctly: "Know then, a man

116. Ibid.
117. Ibid.

can no more carry faith in his heart, and this not reformed his life; then ointment about him, and that not discover it self."[118]

Secondly, true faith will lead to a confession of faith where one is warranted by Christ. Burgess is quick to add that there are points of confession upon which believers might disagree, but on those matters essential to salvation, there can be no equivocation. Those who truly believe must be willing to testify that they are indeed united to Christ by faith.[119] Of particular interest is the fact that Burgess recognizes that the need to confess might occur only under certain circumstances. That is, the believer does not have to confess immediately in order to prove his or her faith, but he or she does have to confess when called upon—particularly in times when persecution is rampant. When called upon, the true Christian must (and will) own up to his or her union with Christ.

Additionally, faith will not only lead to purity and confession when required, it will also lead to obedience to the commands of Christ. As in *Spiritual Refining*, so here Burgess draws upon the words of James:

> *Where faith is, there it will carry a man out to the ready performance of all obedience, justice, temperance, liberality, equity, and every good worke.* The Apostle *James*, Jam 2. doth at large shew, *That that man is but a vain man,* and an hypocrite, one who cousens [unclear in manuscript] his own soul, that thinketh by faith to be saved, when this is not incarnated, and manifested in all godly conversaion: Yea, faith puts all graces on working, as *Heb 11*. That seems to be the great wheel that sets all others on going.[120]

Finally, the last of the *ad extra* effects of true faith is steadfastness in the face of discouragement or trouble. Burgess contrasts faith with worldly fears. It is fear that drives the Christian into sin and faith

118. Ibid., 73.
119. Ibid.
120. Ibid.

that causes him or her to combat such fear. If trouble or discouraging circumstances come, the person with faith can and will overcome; he will not change. As Burgess vividly writes, "A man that liveth by sense, and by worldly advantages, he cannot but with the *chameleon* turn into every colour of that object which is by him, because worldly fear reigneth and ruleth in his heart."[121]

True faith leads to self-examination, with a call to discover whether or not one's conversion is genuine:

> Hath the ministry had this effect to make you believe? Oh, you will say, Who doubts of that? Are we Atheists? Do you make pagans and infidels of us? Consider, there is a great difference between the Title, Name, and Protection of a Believer, and the reall Efficacy of it. It's said, *Simon Magus believed,* because he outwardly *professed* so, yet he was in the state of *gall* and *bitterness.* It's said, *John 2* [unable to read in manuscript]. That *many believed, but Christ would not commit himself to them, because he knew what is in man.* Therefore, Do you really believe all that the Scripture saith? And if so? How darest thou lie, swear, deal unjustly? No: you flatter your selves. The Faith of these things, would make you tremble, yea, roar out: Oh! What shall I do to escape the great wrath! Therefore let Faith work more on, from day to day" I am no Atheist; I am a Christian; I believe a Day of Judgment: Why then live I thus?[122]

Faith is linked to the hearing of the word, and faith is central to the entire life of the Christian. It is more than the instrument of justification and imputed righteousness; it is the ongoing need if the Christian is to resist temptation and overcome fear. And true saving faith will manifest itself in such resistance, if one is truly united with Christ.

121. Ibid.
122. Ibid., 74.

Saving Faith and Assurance

Understanding Burgess's view of faith is critical to understanding his framework for assurance for a number of reasons. For one thing, Burgess believed that, in a certain sense, faith and assurance *should* be found together. The fact that they are not (and he acknowledges they are not) does not imply that they are not deeply intertwined. He writes, "[Faith] is of an establishing and setling Nature. It is a Pillar and an Anchor to the soul, and although Assurance is a separable effect from it, yet the Scripture makes Doubting and Fear to be opposite to believing. Hence is trusting in God compared to rolling ourselves upon him, to staying the minde, to resting of the heart, &c. So that by strong and customary Acts of believing on Christ, and patiently waiting, we come at last to be assured."[123]

Although Burgess here uses the some of the same terminology as Owen, such as "resting" and "waiting," we will see that he clearly intends assurance to be pursued vigorously. Also, as for the question of whether assurance and saving faith are inseparable, Burgess seems to say that though they logically belong together, they are not always found together.

Burgess is quite clear from the beginning of his treatise that assurance is not necessarily found in the heart of every believer, and because of this, it is incumbent upon believers to seek after it. Indeed, Burgess considers it a duty of all believers to seek after assurance. He writes, "For if the heathens did so much admire that saying as an oracle . . . know and be aquanted with your own self, when they had neither true eyes, nor light to discover themselves by, how much rather does this duty lie upon us, when by God's grace we may have the seeing eye, and a sure light of God's word to guide us therein?"[124]

123. Burgess, *Spiritual Refining*, 24.
124. Ibid., 24.

And again, Burgess writes, "*It is a duty of special concernment for the people of God to be assured of such a true and saving work of grace in them, as thereby they shall be differenced from unsound hypocrites. There are certain Notes and Signs of grace, whereby a man may discern what he is.*"[125] For Burgess, seeking after assurance was not an optional part of the Christian life that one could give or take. It was a duty commanded of every believer—one that carried with it great benefits.

But here we also can see three of the main elements of Burgess's teaching regarding the relationship between faith and assurance. First, those who are God's people have a duty to pursue a special assurance of their interest in salvation. This is indicative of Burgess's conviction that, as stated in the WCF, assurance is not a necessary component of saving faith. One can be part of God's people yet not be assured of being classified as such. Second, we see here that Burgess envisions the possibility—perhaps even the probability—of unsound hypocrites having a false measure of assurance. That is, he believes there are some who incorrectly assume they have a saving interest in the work of Christ, when in fact they are mistaken in this. (This, incidentally, is a key and distinctive feature of Burgess's writings on the topic of assurance; as such, it will be dealt with in the following chapter.) Third, and perhaps most importantly for our purposes in this chapter, we see that Burgess is persuaded that certain signs accompany saving faith. These signs are intended to be used to give assurance to individual Christians and to God's people corporately. The believer (or congregation) works backward from the true evidences of grace in his or her life; from these, believers can assert with confidence that they have a saving interest in Christ.

This point sharply distinguishes Burgess's approach from the approach followed by Owen and Goodwin. Their approach seems to

---

125. Ibid., 2 (italics in original).

become the standard way of expanding upon the WCF for pastoral and other needs. But Burgess's approach, while not perhaps conflicting with theirs, nonetheless has a decidedly different focus. This is not the only area in which his expansions on the Westminster consensus differed from those proposed by others in their writings.

Burgess's Framework of True Assurance

One of the questions raised in the reading of the WCF statement on assurance relates to the true signs of saving faith. The WCF holds out the possibility of certainty in the matter of one's faith, and the divines were even explicit that this could be attained through regular means and obeying the dictates of a pure conscience. But what exactly these regular means consist of, and what it means to act in a way consistent with a pure conscience are not spelled out. Put another way, the WCF affirms that true ("infallible") assurance is possible, but it only sketches out in the most general way just what kind of life might lead to that absolute assurance. Burgess addresses this specifically: "Now in these ways the people of God come to have assurance: 1. *By a deep and serious humiliation for sin, and feeling the burden of it* . . . . 2. *Another method whereby God worketh assurance, is by conflicts of doubts, and opposition of unbelief.* . . . 3. *God worketh assurance out of the vehement and fiery assaults of Satan.*"[126]

Burgess's introductory sentence assumes that God's people may lack assurance. There is no sense here that they had it and lost it, but rather that, though regenerate, they had never enjoyed it. Also, Burgess, unlike the WCF itself, is addressing straightaway not just the reality of distinguishing between faith and assurance, nor simply

---

126. Ibid., 19–20.

the value of assurance, but the actual way in which it is achieved in the life of the believer. This leads to Burgess's great emphasis.

Burgess's ultimate contention is that being assured of one's present sanctification is the means by which one receives assurance about the other privileges of salvation. He writes, "*There are four special priviledges and mercies that a Christian even in this life may be assured of, his Election, Remission of sinne, Sanctification of his nature, and Perseverance in that state, with future glory at the end thereof.* And the assurance of our Sanctification or present grace must be the foundation for the other certainties; so that there can be no certainty of Predestination, or Justification, of Glorification, if there be not a certainty of Renovation in us."[127]

For Burgess, the main objective with respect to assurance must be to ascertain whether one is showing the true marks of sanctification. We have noted already that he is clear on the fact that sanctification itself is the result of justification, so there is no question here of altering the basic *ordo salutis* (order of salvation). Rather, the question relates to how one gains an enduring and reliable assurance of justification. For this, the marks of sanctification are essential. These marks are the evidence from which one can work backward into a determination of whether one is elect, or forgiven of one's sins, or whether one will inherit future glory. The great duty associated with assurance is the duty to examine one's own Christian experience, to test whether or not one is bearing the true fruit of salvation.

Like Goodwin, Burgess presents two levels of believers, though unlike Goodwin, these are not presented with any reference to the sealing of the Spirit. Burgess writes these words on the parable of the two builders in Matt. 7:24-6: "What is represented, but two kinds of believers, one that has the outward profession and way

---

127. Ibid., 19.

of Christianity, and he is also truly *rooted upon Christ*; but there is another who builds upon the sand, who digs not deep enough."[128] There are believers who are not assured of their faith, not because they have yet to receive some special dispensation of miraculous grace or to commune more deeply with God in his triune essence. Rather, they have not dug deeply enough into the roots of who they are in Christ. They have not looked closely enough at the work of Christ, which is bearing fruit in their lives despite their lack of attention to it. It is inattention to Christ's work in particular that keeps them from the assurance they desperately need.

So believers, in Burgess's estimation, are commanded to dig deeply into their lives for assurance. Burgess writes this: "Now when the apostle commands us *to prove and try ourselves*, it is to endeavor to feel that in actual working, which we persuade ourselves is in us habitually."[129] Then, in the same paragraph, "The Scripture in Philippians 1:9 calls this *sense* or *feeling*, where the Apostle distinguishes it from *knowledge* and *judgement*, making it to be the inward savoury sense and feeling of divine things upon their hearts."[130] Burgess enjoins people to seek out an inward sense of assurance; he describes this inward sense of assurance as clearly as Owen or Goodwin. But the inward sense, for Burgess, is something believers gain by carefully observing of the fruit of sanctification.

As Burgess's treatise on assurance progresses, these themes come out even more clearly. Burgess addresses the question "What are the characteristical differences between assurance and presumption?"[131] This question quite naturally emerges from his framework for gaining assurance. And when defining assurance, he writes,

128. Ibid., 4.
129. Ibid., 3.
130. Ibid.
131. Ibid., 16.

"Assurance is a fruit, whose root is in heaven, the Spirit of God in a two-fold act, enlightening or revealing, and adopting or corroborating the heart with filial evangelical affections; but carnal presumption is a rush that grows in the puddled mire of our own hearts; There being these internal causes that give life and breath to it."[132]

It should also be noted (though it goes slightly beyond the object of our study) that, as we have already alluded to, assurance for Burgess is not merely a personal matter; it can be corporate. That is, Burgess conceives of his teaching on assurance as relating not only to individuals who have need of assurance, but also to congregations. An individual needs to be assured of his or her saving interest in Christ, but a congregation needs to be assured that it is a true congregation of Christ. While introducing this category of assurance, Burgess quickly notes that this assurance is much easier to attain than personal assurance: "*It is easier for a particular Church to know it is a true visible Church, than for a particular Christian to know that he is a true believer.* For to a true visible Church are required only those notes and marks which are external, as the pure preaching of the Word with an external submission unto it, or receiving of it, and where this is, a man may conclude there is a true visible Church for the essence of it."[133]

Aside from the peculiar notion of the Westminster doctrine of assurance being applied corporately (a notion not heretofore observed in Owen, Goodwin, or others), this quote is of interest for other reasons. It shows us once again the manner in which Burgess is inclined to argue for assurance. He makes his case by describing the things that would mark out a genuine work of God and instructs

132. Ibid.
133. Ibid., 18.

those seeking assurance to draw it from their observation and analysis of this evidence.

In essence, Burgess's reasoning could be summarized by this simple syllogism: *Major Premise:* Those who are regenerate evidence particular characteristics. *Minor Premise:* I evidence those same characteristics. *Conclusion:* Therefore, I am regenerate. This is a helpful summary of Burgess's approach. The substance of his treatise is necessarily focused on how to fill in the major premise of this syllogism—that is, what particular characteristics of sanctification prove, when present, that an individual is saved.

Because of this focus, Burgess's work is essentially an attempt to expound the various types of obedience that may rightly be considered means of grace—namely, love and abstinence from and resistance to sin.[134] This very basic connection between obedience and saving grace is founded on two fundamental principles: "The knowledge of God makes us to keep God's commandments," and, "Observation of God's commandments is a sign by way of an effect, to assure us that we know God, which is the cause."[135]   This language of cause and effect and of observation of the effect leading us back to the cause is typical of Burgess. He is operating from a series of premises. These are what the believer can use to gain an inward sense of assurance. And these premises are possible only because of Burgess's definition of faith.

It should be said that most of the work, at least in volume 1, is taken up with showing the things that are *not* true signs (showing what evidence is *not* a true sign must be distinguished from the things that are evidences that someone is *not* regenerate.) This is precisely what one might expect if the syllogistic framework is foundational. Burgess must address not only the things that mark out true

134. Ibid., 33, 41.
135. Ibid., 24.

sanctifying grace, but also which might be normally considered signs of grace but are, in his estimation, inconclusive. In this, his sermon titles are a useful guide:

- Gifts and Parts in Matters of Religion, No Sign of Grace;
- Fully Clearing That There May be Affections and Sweet Motions of Heart in Holy Things, Which Yet Evidence Not Grace, Nor Accompany Salvation;
- Manifesting That the Greatest Sufferings for Christ Are Not Infallible Evidences of Grace;
- Showing that, and Whence Men Have Such Strong Persuasions of their Exact Keeping of God's Law;
- External Obedience to the Law of God No Sure Evidence for Heaven;
- That Every Peaceable Frame of Heart, and Persuasion of God's Love, Is Not a Sure Testimony of Saving Grace;
- That Outward Success, Prosperity, and Greatness in the World is No True Evidence of Grace;
- That a Man's Leaving those Gross Sins He Hath Lived in Is No Sign of Grace.[136]

While these will need to be explored in greater detail in the next chapter, where we shall expand in greater detail upon the specific evidences of assurance that Burgess discusses, the fact that these kinds of false signs play such a large part in Burgess's understanding of assurance tells us something. From their central place, we see what key questions Burgess was asking. It could be said that Burgess fills out the WCF by his use of syllogisms. And with this syllogistic framework firmly in view, he then explores how believers can

---

136. Ibid., table of contents.

correctly assess whether the works in their life bear the mark of genuine sanctification.

This is not Burgess's only focus. He is emphatic in his attention to Christ's promises: "It cannot be denied but that it is a more noble and excellent way to believe in the Promise than to believe upon the sense and evidences of Grace in us, yet this latter is also lawful and encouraged by God."[137] However, as a practical matter, Burgess paid far more attention in his writings to the use of syllogisms for ascertaining assurance. It was the evidence that led one back to the promise. Burgess no doubt would have considered this a response to his pastoral situation and the needs of his congregation. After all, he was nothing if not pastorally minded. But we can see that even Owen and Goodwin, who were driven by similar pastoral concerns, handled the matter differently.

Conclusion

The WCF laid some important groundwork for understanding the doctrine of assurance. However, even among those who agreed with its general outline, there was need for further expansion. Anthony Burgess was among those who set to work expanding upon it, but he did so in distinctive ways.

Burgess's framework calls into question some basic assumptions about the post-Reformation developments in this area. Beeke, for instance, writes this about the post-Reformation formulations of assurance: "As an outgrowth of Calvin and the early Reformers' views on assurance, the post-Reformers further developed the doctrine of assurance—both pastorally and theologically—moving it from a Christological to a Trinitarian framework."[138]

---

137. Quoted in Beeke, "Anthony Burgess on Assurance," 34.

Perhaps this is true in some measure in Burgess: he certainly does believe that assurance is ultimately a work of the Holy Spirit, though it is mediated through attention to God's word and to the works of the Spirit in the life of the believer. In that sense, his focus is pneumatological only secondarily. And as we will see, this emphasis that Beeke notes does not appear as clearly in Burgess as in Owen or Goodwin. Burgess prioritizes the objective work of Christ on behalf of the believer as the source of assurance, and he also pays extensive attention to the ongoing, sanctifying work of the Holy Spirit as evidence. But this is not a mystical exercise in communion with the Holy Spirit; rather, as one looks to good works done for good reasons and not out of hypocrisy, one can infer certain things about the work of the Holy Spirit. Burgess is certainly aware that this, in itself, is difficult to decipher, given the deceptiveness of the human heart.

It is possible that this type of emphasis may reflect something of the influence of Theodore Beza. Beza emphasized the use of syllogisms in reaching an assurance of one's faith. Beeke quotes Graafland's summary of Beza in this regard: "To these acts Beza reckons, in the very first place, sanctification, which is begun in us and consists of a hatred of sin and a love for righteousness. Secondly, Beza speaks of the witness of the Holy Spirit, which encourages my conscience. It appears that these two acts of the Spirit are so clearly recognizable that they can form a ground which enables us to ascertain and be assured of our faith and election."[139]

Beeke again writes of the post-WCF theologians, "As a rule, the divines exemplified a healthy, Pauline mysticism that was Word-regulated with a Christ-centered and Trinitarian matrix."[140] There is no question that Burgess fits the description "Word-regulated" and

---

138. Joel R. Beeke, *The Quest for Full Assurance: The Legacy of Calvin and His Successors* (Edinburgh: Banner of Truth, 1999), 274.
139. *De zekerheid van het geloof*, p. 69, quoted in Beeke, *Quest*, 77.
140. Beeke, *Quest*, 275.

"Christ-centered," but whether he had a "mysticism" of the type seen elsewhere is not self-evident. What is in fact most striking is the way in which Burgess employs syllogistic reasoning when addressing the topic. Burgess aims at the concrete and discursive.

It should come as no surprise that Burgess often uses syllogistic reasoning when formulating his conclusions. His education, from its very earliest years, was intent on making men adept at the use of this kind of logical analysis and rhetorical presentation.[141] To indicate that this is ipso facto evidence of a departure from Calvin, as some have asserted, seems to confuse theological method with theological content, at least in Burgess's case. While Burgess's *method* is often based on syllogisms and his rhetoric employs syllogisms vigorously, this is not the same thing as saying his content is governed by certain core presuppositions, which must then be defended on rationalistic grounds. In fact, the figure who emerges in a study of Burgess's framework for assurance is not that of a cold rationalist, but that of a concrete realist. He seems to be attempting to systematize what he believes to be the natural pastoral outworking of the doctrines in the text of Scripture. Because good works are the normal and necessary outcome of saving faith, believers can work backward from those works to assure themselves of the reality of Christ's union with them.

For Burgess, receiving assurance of one's faith is an element of the ministry of the word. It is through the word of God that one receives Christ's promises; it is through the word that one understands what true faith looks like, giving one the opportunity to work backward from the fruit of sanctification to the root of justification. The preached word can bring about faith and assurance, empowered, as it is, by God the Holy Spirit. All this, even faith, is a gift of Christ.[142] From hearing to faith to assurance, the Christian's interpretation

---

141. See chapter 1.
142. Burgess, *Spiritual Refining*, 71.

of his or her spiritual life is to be governed by a proper attention to God's word. Burgess writes, "That which is the means of our regeneration, is also of our assurance, *that we through the Scriptures might have comfort.*"[143]

143. Ibid., 17 (italics in original).

4

Further Development

The Framework for Assurance in Thomas Goodwin
and John Owen

We have spent considerable time introducing Anthony Burgess. But he serves not only as one key figure in our study, but rather as a kind of introductory figure in our study of post-Westminster writing on assurance in general. The three categories we examined for Burgess—Puritan, pastor, and scholar—are the relevant lenses through which to view the other figures in our study as well. Primarily our objective is to show that all three of these men (Burgess, Thomas Goodwin, and John Owen) fit into the same basic categories as we established in the Burgess biography. In addition, my goal is to demonstrate that each of the three would have readily assented to the Westminster consensus on assurance. The point in studying them is to show the immediate fault lines that developed among those who shared these basic similarities in background and theological orientation.

Goodwin and Owen: Puritans, Pastors, Scholars

Anthony Burgess was not the only theologian and writer of his day who both agreed with the Westminster consensus and sought to either clarify it or expand upon it. In fact, both Thomas Goodwin and John Owen did the same thing. These two men are better known, so we can deal with their biographical details more briefly than we did with Burgess.

Background of Thomas Goodwin

There is reason to believe that Thomas Goodwin may have grown up in what would be considered a Puritan home. As Hanbury points out, there was a predominance of Puritanism in the area in which Goodwin was raised (eastern Norfolk) during the early 1600s.[1] Goodwin, who was born in Rollesby in October 1600, would have certainly been exposed to this kind of teaching.

If we cannot say with certainty that Goodwin's parents were interested in ecclesiastical reform in the Puritan mold, we can say that they encouraged him both in his Christian faith generally and in his call to the ministry more specifically. He is said to have been acquainted with the Scriptures from infancy and to have been set apart for the work of gospel ministry from boyhood.[2]

Goodwin recalls experiencing a work of the Holy Spirit through his emotions as early as the age of six. He experienced anguish and deep sorrow over the thought of his own sin, and deep joy over thoughts of God.[3] What is especially striking is the way in

---

1. Benjamin Hanbury, *Historical Memorials Relating to the Independents or Congregationalists* (London: Fisher, 1839), 1:14.
2. Thomas Goodwin, *Works* (Edinburgh: James Nichol, 1861), 2:xi.
3. Ibid., 2:xiii.

which Goodwin later incorporated deep emotional experiences into his doctrine of the work of the Holy Spirit in assurance.

Goodwin's educational background also underscores his commitment to Puritanism. He entered Christ's College, Cambridge, at the age of twelve. Goodwin seems to have found at least six fellows at college who went over Ursin's catechism with interested students on Saturday nights, and in addition, Goodwin listened to the sermons of Richard Sibbes, who was preaching at Trinity Parish Church at the time.[4] At the age of fourteen, Goodwin first prepared to take Communion. In the time leading up to this, Goodwin sought to examine himself closely. What he found was a heart filled with rapture and joy at the things of God. He read Calvin's *Institutes* as part of his preparation and remarked, "How sweet was the reading of some parts of that book for me."[5]

Nonetheless, he was dissuaded from taking Communion by a tutor, Mr. Power, who thought he was not ready. Goodwin became quite bitter, stopped going to hear Sibbes, and began to seek after personal glory.[6] He graduated with a bachelor of arts degree at sixteen.

In 1620, he was elected a fellow of Catherine Hall, and in October of that year, he happened upon the funeral procession of a friend. He followed the procession to hear the funeral sermon. In Goodwin's own words, "The matter of the sermon was vehemently urged on the hearer not to let slip the opportunity of that day, but immediately to turn to God and to defer no longer; being edged with that direful threatening, lest if he did not turn to God in that day, the day of grace and salvation, it might eternally be hid from his eyes."[7] It is interesting to note, considering his views on assurance, that Goodwin

4. Ibid., 2:lix.
5. Ibid., 2:lii.
6. Ibid.
7. Ibid., 2:liv.

examined his own experience and listed four reasons why he was confident in the genuineness of his faith. First, he saw the change come to him in a time when his heart was otherwise hardened; the change and the message came at the proper time and place for him; the promise he received was the one received by Paul and therefore sufficient for his sins also; and finally, his new life proved that the conversion had been real.[8] Brown states that one of the outcomes of Goodwin's conversion and reflection upon his conversion "was the ability to help people in their struggle for assurance."[9]

In 1628, Goodwin succeeded John Preston, who had himself followed Richard Sibbes. Goodwin occupied this pastoral post until the Laudian purge of 1634; from 1639 to 1641, Goodwin lived in exile in the Netherlands. He was to return and play a significant role in the formulation of the Westminster Confession of Faith (WCF) and later to work with John Owen on further doctrinal formulations that related to assurance.

Whatever else we might say about Goodwin (and there remains a great deal more in his autobiographical accounts), we can certainly say that he fits the three categories we have established for Anthony Burgess. Goodwin would certainly fit our definition of a Puritan, was a pastor from the very earliest days after his conversion, and certainly had a Scholastic background that, in method and rigor, resembles Burgess's own. Since these categories are the ones through which we have been viewing Burgess, one might expect Burgess and Goodwin to have identical views on the matter of assurance. As we will see, however, this is not the case.

8. Paul E. Brown, "The Principle of the Covenant in the Theology of Thomas Goodwin" (PhD diss., Drew University, Madison, NJ, 1950), 14.
9. Ibid., 15.

Background of John Owen

John Owen was born in 1616 in Oxfordshire into a nonconformist family. Although we know little about his grammar school education, we do know that it prepared him to enter Queen's College, graduating with a bachelor of arts degree from Oxford University at age sixteen.[10] Among other things, we know that he took part in the debates at Oxford and received the requisite training in grammar and rhetoric.[11] In 1635, he earned his master's degree and began to study for his Bacehlor of Divinity, also having been ordained as a deacon by John Bancroft.[12]

Because of the orders of Charles I regarding debates about issues such as election and predestination, Owen eventually came to see that he would have to leave university life. This is a sign of his early convictions on these matters, and he left Oxford University in 1637 to become chaplain to Sir William Dormer and then, shortly after this, chaplain to John Lord Lovelace.[13] Upon the eruption of the civil war in 1642, Owen left Lovelace, who was a supporter of the king, and moved to London.[14] Though he was not part of the Westminster Assembly, it is notable that in 1643, the House of Commons ordered the printing of his book *A Display of Arminianism*, which Owen dedicated to the Committee on Religion of the House of Lords. In 1644, his second book, *The Duties of Pastors and People*, was published.

Owen's own experience of assurance came while in London during that time. He admits to lacking assurance, perhaps for as many as five years prior to his arrival.[15] He went to hear Edmund

---

10. Sinclair Ferguson, *John Owen and the Christian Life* (Edinburgh: Banner of Truth, 1987), 1.
11. Ibid.
12. Ibid., 2.
13. Richard L. Greaves, *Oxford Dictionary of National Biography*, online at http://www.oxforddnb.com, s.v. "John Owen."
14. Ibid.

Calumny speak at Aldermanbury Chapel, but there was a substitute preacher instead. However, Owen records this as the moment when he experienced personally God's love shed in his heart.[16] His experience was intense and apparently unabated from that time forward.

When we look at Owen through the grid established with Burgess and Goodwin, we see he fits well into all three categories. He was certainly a Puritan and often served in pastoral roles, and some of his earliest written work concerned pastoral theology. Finally, like both Goodwin and Burgess, Owen was trained in the Scholasticism of the day. Although it must be noted that we know next to nothing about his grammar school, we can see the same type of training in logic and syllogisms for Owen as we saw for the other two.

Both Goodwin and Owen provide ideal standards for comparing with Burgess. Their associations and sympathies are largely the same as his. They have deeply pastoral concerns and are both thoughtful analysts of the duties of pastoral ministry. And like Burgess, they were trained to think, write, and debate, in the same basic ways. As we will see, all three agreed with the Westminster consensus on assurance, but their expansions after the WCF provide helpful insight into both the nature of the WCF and the variegated ways in which Puritans equally committed to it could apply its formulations. In looking at these three figures, we have provided some control for our study, seeking to answer this question: How did these three figures, all of whom agreed with the Westminster consensus, differ so sharply on the matter of assurance—an area in which the WCF is rightly recognized as providing definition and clarity unlike what we find in any of the previous Protestant confessions?

---

15. Ferguson, *John Owen*, 2.
16. Ibid.

Areas of Agreement on Assurance

Thomas Goodwin and John Owen agreed on several matters regarding assurance of salvation. Like Burgess, Owen and Goodwin broadly affirmed the WCF and its formulation on the doctrine of assurance. But also like Burgess, they each made statements that sought to further define or explain the WCF.

Owen's View of Assurance in His Catechisms

Most of our understanding of Owen's view of assurance comes from his commentary on Psalm 130. However, his two catechisms from 1645 also address his explanation of the question of true faith and, to some degree, the assurance of that true faith.[17]

The catechisms are of particular interest first, because they were written the earliest. Note that 1645, the year in which the catechisms were published, was before the publication of the Westminster Confession of Faith. In fact, the debate among the divines about the precise language of the WCF on assurance did not take place until September 1646.[18] In his catechisms (called "Lesser" and "Greater," respectively), Owen answers two questions about the nature of faith that have a bearing on our understanding of his views of assurance:

Q: *What is a lively faith?*

A: An assured resting of the soul upon God's promises of mercy in Jesus Christ, for pardon of sins here and in glory.[19]

---

17. Quotations from Owen's catechisms are taken from *The Works of John Owen*, ed. William H. Goold, repr. ed. (Edinburgh: Banner of Truth, 1967) (hereafter Owen, *Works*).
18. See Chad Van Dixhoorn, "Reforming the Reformation: Theological Debate at the Westminster Assembly, 1643-1652" (PhD Dissertation, Cambridge University, 2004) 6:335
19. Owen, *Works*, 1:468. (lesser catechism)

His second question and answer are even more significant:

Q. 2. *What is a justifying faith?*

A gracious resting upon the free promises of God in Jesus Christ for mercy, with a firm persuasion of the heart that God is a reconciled Father unto us in the Son of his love.[20]

We will have to return to these specific statements later when evaluating the effect that the consensus at Westminster had on Owen's later apparent modification of these views, but for now, it is worth noting several things about them. First, in both, Owen refers to faith as a resting upon God's promises in Jesus Christ. As we will see, this definition of true faith bears a great resemblance to Goodwin's. It is a remarkably clear rejection of any kind of salvation by works, which, as we will see, Goodwin also works strenuously to refute.

Second, we cannot help but notice that in the first question, Owen refers to faith as "an assured resting," and in the second as "a firm persuasion from the heart that God is a reconciled Father *unto us* [emphasis, JLM]." It would seem at first glance as if these earlier works of Owen combined the notion of assurance with that of saving faith. Beeke comments on this feature of Owen's statements this way: "First, they reveal Owen's earlier conviction that assurance is part and parcel of faith. . . . Did the assembly's documents have a direct bearing on his reorientation? Or did this shift take place through a more complicated process involving theological maturation, personal experience, and pastoral contacts with parishioners who appeared simultaneously to possess faith and lack full assurance?"[21]

---

20. Owen, *Works*, 1:486. (greater catechism)
21. Joel Beeke, *Assurance of Faith: Calvin, English Puritanism, and the Dutch Second Reformation* (New York: Peter Lang, 1994), 213–14.

One hesitates slightly in reaching this tentative conclusion about Owen's early writing. First, although both statements mention assurance in some way, it is entirely possible that the use of the term, at least in the first statement, in its context is different from the meaning intended by the WCF. While in the first statement, from the "Lesser Catechism," Owen speaks of faith in terms of "assured resting," the assurance he speaks of seems to be confidence in the reliability of God's promises in Christ. Further, while the statement from the "Great Catechism" (the second one quoted) is perhaps clearer than the first in terms of being assured that Christ's work is being appropriated to the individual believer, it is still worth considering whether this is the same kind of thing that the WCF addresses. Is what Owen describes an inward full and sure persuasion that God's promises of salvation in Christ are effectual for *each believer as an individual*? Perhaps it is. But his lack of further explanation, combined with the use of the term *us*, may give some cause to wonder. In any case, it is enough for our purposes to note that this early statement of Owen's is not one that fits easily with the writings of Anthony Burgess on the topic, and it rests somewhat uneasily with the WCF formulation written at approximately the same time—a formulation that Owen played no role in writing.[22]

22. One reason for the tentativeness of my conclusions regarding the supposed dissonance between Owen's catechisms and the WCF is the spiritual biography of Owen himself. Owen struggled mightily with assurance, though he had faith, from about 1637 to 1643. It is difficult for one to reconcile this with the assumption that he considered absolute assurance, of the kind referenced in the WCF, to be an essential feature of saving faith—especially in 1645. For an introduction to this, see Beeke, *Assurance of Faith*, 239–40. See also Dewey Wallace Jr., "The Life and Thought of John Owen to 1660: A Study of the Significance of Calvinist Theology in English Puritanism" (PhD diss., Princeton University, 1962).

Owen's View of Assurance in His Polemical Writings

As Owen progresses (and perhaps as the consensus reached in the WCF takes hold), he elaborates more fully on the doctrine of assurance. This happens in the context of a polemical dispute with John Goodwin (not to be confused with Thomas Goodwin, whose writings we will explore in short order). His dispute with Goodwin relates to the doctrine of perseverance. In short, Goodwin believed that true believers can fall from the grace of salvation. The possibility of apostasy for true believers was not merely hypothetical for Goodwin; it was real. It is beyond the scope of this study to detail this dispute, but it is worth noting the statements on assurance that Owen makes in his 1654 response entitled *The Doctrine of the Saints' Perseverance*.[23] Here we see Owen either develop or clarify his earlier positions on assurance.

In this treatise, Owen confirms that assurance is something that grows in the life of the believer. In fact, he seems to take this growth in assurance for granted, writing, "That the Scripture builds up our assurance on other foundations is evident, and the saints acknowledge it."[24] Owen also adds a statement that is rather confusing but may hint at the distinction between his earlier statement in the "Greater Catechism" about assurance and his agreement with the formulations of the WCF; in fact, he seems here to echo the language of the confession:

> I no way doubt but many thousands of believers, whose apprehension of the nature, properties, and conditions of things, as they are in themselves, are low, weak, and confused, yet, having received the Spirit of adoption, bearing witness with their spirits that they are children of God, and having the testimony in themselves, have been taken up into

23. This can be found in Owen, *Works*, 11:1–666. This is the edition that will be referenced throughout.
24. Owen, *Works*, 11:84.

as high a degree of comforting and cheering assurance, and that upon the most infallible foundation imaginable (for 'the Spirit beareth witness, because the Spirit is truth,' 1 John v.6), as ever the most seraphically illuminated person in the world attained unto.[25]

It is striking to note that Owen's understanding of "the most infallible foundation imaginable" consists of the inward witness of the Holy Spirit with the spirit of the believer. Too, his use of the term "infallible" with "assurance" indicates a possible connection in his mind with the WCF. There is also here his acknowledgment that a believer's apprehension of things can be, and often is, "low, weak, and confused."[26] This is echoed in a statement he makes in the same treatise, when he writes, "Neither is the spiritual confidence of the saints shaken, much less cast to the ground, by their conflicting with fears, scruples, and doubtful apprehensions."[27] Though the tone of this statement is notably hopeful, indicating the believer's overcoming of these internal conflicts, it is no less significant for that: Owen understands that internal confidence may be mixed with, and even overwhelmed by, confusion. And to strike another note from the WCF, Owen also gives pride of place to the kind of assurance produced by the internal witness of the Spirit, calling this the "most infallible [assurance] imaginable."

Goodwin and Owen: Assurance through Communion with God

It is worth noting at this point the important ways in which both Owen and Goodwin expanded upon the WCF in exploring the doctrine of assurance.[28] One of the most profound of these expansions

25. Ibid., 11:82.
26. Ibid, 11:82
27. Ibid., 11:83.
28. I am indebted to Beeke's analysis of Owen's position on assurance, from which I derived several of the quotations contained in this section from Owen's *Works*. Though I am not

came in the way they connected the Christian's assurance of faith with his or her communion with the triune God. We will begin with a quote from Goodwin that will make this connection clear:

> It is in assurance: sometimes a man's communion and converse is with the one, sometimes with the other; sometimes with the Father, then with the Son, and then with the Holy Ghost; sometimes his heart is drawn out to consider the Father's love in choosing, and then the love of Christ in redeeming, and so again the love of the Holy Ghost, that searcheth the deep things of God, and revealeth them to us, and taketh all the pains with us; and so a man goes from one witness to another distinctly, which, I say, is the communion that John would have us to have. . . . And this assurance it is not a knowledge by way of argument or deduction, whereby we infer that if one loveth me than the other loveth me, but it is intuitively, as I may so express it, and we should never be satisfied till we have attained it, and till all three persons lie level in us, and all make their abode with us, and we sit as it were in the midst of them, while they all manifest their love unto us.[29]

Here we can see one of the keystones of both Thomas Goodwin's and John Owen's primary approaches to this matter of assurance. Both of them emphasized that assurance is given to the believer through the means of communion with the Persons of the Trinity in their personal distinctiveness. That is, the believer must engage with the Father, Son, and Spirit in their distinctive economic roles, and complete assurance will involve comprehending the love of all three Persons particularly. As we will see, though this quote comes from Goodwin, it fairly represents Owen's position as well. Before showing this, however, it is also worth noting two additional things about this statement. First, Goodwin (and Owen too, at this point) views assurance as something that needs to be gained as one moves

---

fully persuaded of all the particular conclusions he reaches, especially regarding Owen's earliest formulations, I owe a great deal to his thoughtful work. See especially Beeke, *Assurance of Faith*, 215–70.

29. Goodwin, *Works*, 8:378–79.

forward in the Christian life. The kind of assurance mentioned here is clearly not something the believer attains immediately upon his or her conversion. It is something that is pursued, waited for, reflected upon. Further, it is quite striking to note that the assurance given through this communion is *contrasted* with "knowledge by way of argument or deduction." This is especially relevant to bear in mind as we consider the work of Anthony Burgess. Having observed his early training as a thinker, we will not be surprised that Burgess advocates a pursuit of assurance—and an identification of its presence or absence—based quite firmly on a syllogistic footing.

The way this works out in Owen's understanding is that the believer must commune with the Father to apprehend the Father's love. The believer, through Christ, is, "brought into the bosom of God, into a comfortable persuasion, and spiritual perception and sense of his love, there reposes and rests itself."[30] Elsewhere, Owen writes on this communion with the Father, "If thou believest and receives the Father as love, he will infallibly be so to thee."[31]

With respect to the Son, Beeke identifies two ways in which Owen advises the believer to commune with him. First, Owen can refer to this communion as a kind of marriage—or, as Beeke calls it, a "conjugal relation."[32] Incidentally, Burgess also uses the language of marriage when describing the believer's relation to Christ. But for Burgess, it is faith that brings about the union, whereas, for Owen, the conjugal relation is a description of the communion one must strive to have.

Perhaps more importantly for Owen than the metaphor of marriage is the apprehension of Christ's work of adoption. Owen affirms that the believer's adoption, with Christ as the elder brother,

---

30. Owen, *Works*, 2:22.
31. Ibid., 2:37.
32. Beeke, *Assurance of Faith*, 226.

begins immediately upon his conversion, "with his investiture in all the privileges and advantages of that family."[33] But as one communes with the Son as an elder brother, examining and meditating on the many ways in which his role in this capacity is worked out, one gains further assurance of his particular love. In essence, what Owen argues is that the all the benefits of adoption, including boldness, access to the Father, and confident hope for a future inheritance, are included in God's initial work of adoption in Christ. But it is only as the believer contemplates this, communing with Christ the elder brother, that he can fully appreciate its significance. Owen writes, "But believers have it always in the root and principle, even all that have received the Spirit of adoption, and are ordinarily assisted in the use of it."[34]

Finally, the believer must commune with the Spirit. This is perhaps the element of communion with God that has the most direct bearing on the question of Owen's view of assurance. He draws his analysis from the text of Rom. 8:16, a principal scriptural proof used also in the WCF. He is worth quoting in full:

> Another effect we have of his, Rom viii. 16, 'The Spirit itself beareth witness with our spirit, that we are the children of God.' You know whose children we are by nature; – children of Satan and of the curse, or of wrath. By the Spirit we are put into another capacity, and are adopted to be the children of God, inasmuch as by receiving the Spirit of our Father we become the children of our Father. Thence is he called, verse 15, 'The Spirit of adoption.' Now, sometimes the soul, because it hath somewhat remaining in it the principle that it had in its old condition, is put to question whether it be a child of God or no; and with all the evidences that it hath to make good its title. The Spirit comes and bears witness in this case. An allusion it is to judicial proceedings in point of titles and evidences. The judge being set, the person concerned lays his claim, produceth his evidences, and pleads

33. Owen, *Works*, 2:279.
34. Ibid., 2:294.

them; his adversaries endeavoring all that in them lies to invalidate them, and disannul his plea, and to cast him in his claim. In the midst of the trial, a person of known and approved integrity comes into the court, and gives testimony fully and directly on the behalf of the claimer; which stops the mouths of all his adversaries, and fills the man that pleaded with joy and satisfaction. So it is in this case. The soul, by the power of its own conscience, is brought before the law of God. There a man puts in his plea, – that he is a child of God, that he belongs to God's family; and for this end produceth all his evidences, every thing whereby faith gives him an interest in God. Satan, in the meantime, opposeth with all his might; sin and law assist him; many flaws are found in his evidences; the truth of them all is questioned; and the soul hangs in suspense as to the issue. In the midst of the plea and contest the Comforter comes, and, by a word of promise or otherwise, overpowers the heart with a comfortable persuasion (and bears down all objections) that his plea is good, and that he is a child of God. And therefore it is said of him, Συμμαρτυρεῖ τῷ πνεύματι ἡμῶν. When our spirits are pleading their right and title, he comes in and hears witness on our side; at the same time enabling us to put forth acts of filial obedience, kind and child-like; which is called 'crying, Abba, Father,' Gal. iv. 6. Remember still the manner of the Spirit's working, before mentioned, – that he doth it effectually, voluntarily, and freely. Hence, sometimes the dispute hangs long, – the cause is pleading many years. The law seems sometime to prevail, sin and Satan to rejoice; and the poor soul is filled with dread about its inheritance. Perhaps its own witness, from its faith, sanctification, former experience, keeps up the plea with some life and comfort; but the work is not done, the conquest not fully obtained, until the Spirit, who worketh freely and effectually, when and how he will, comes in with his testimony also; clothing his power with a word of promise, he makes all parties concerned to attend unto him, and puts an end to the controversy.

Herein he gives us holy communion with himself. The soul knows his voice when he speaks, 'Nec hominem sonat.' There is something too great in it to be the effect of a created power. When the Lord Jesus at one word stilled the raging of the sea and wind, all that were with him knew there was divine power at hand, Matt viii. 25-27. And when the Holy Ghost by one word stills the tumults and storms that are raised in the soul, giving it an immediate claim and security, it knows his divine power, and rejoices in his presence.[35]

The Savoy Declaration

Perhaps this long quote will serve as an appropriate transition to Owen and Goodwin's formulation in the Savoy Declaration. Although we cannot be certain which of them contributed the precise wording in each case, we can say that the Savoy statement was endorsed by both, and both had a hand in its writing. For this 1658 document, they adopt nearly all the language of the WCF. Beeke has a helpful quotation of the Savoy statement on assurance, with the changes italicized. It corresponds directly with WCF 18.2: "This certainty is not a bare conjectural and probable persuasion, grounded upon a fallible hope, but an infallible assurance of faith, founded *on the blood and righteousness of Christ, revealed in the Gospel, and also upon* the inward evidence of those graces unto which promises are made, *and on the immediate witness* of the Spirit, *testifying to our* Adoption, and *as a fruit thereof, leaving the heart more humble and holy*" (italics added to indicate changes from the WCF).[36]

The Savoy Declaration in most respects follows the precise wording of the WCF. The first change (indicated in italics) seems designed to further reinforce that it is Christ's blood that secures righteousness, not any person's works. The second change is perhaps more significant, since it moves from the Westminster language more abruptly. Here we see the change from "the testimony of the Spirit" to "and the immediate witness of the Spirit." Perhaps this change was intended as a clarification of what the WCF meant all along, but Beeke suggests that it is intended to draw a distinction between the inward evidence of graces and another inward work, this one immediate.[37] This does at least seem plausible and would

---

35. Owen, *Works*, 2:241–42.
36. Quoted with italics in Beeke, *Assurance of Faith*, 237.
37. Beeke, *Assurance of Faith*, 238.

reflect Goodwin's and Owen's dominant emphasis on assurance, namely, immediate inward apprehension of God's salvation.

There is also the addition of the category of adoption. This comes as no surprise, given the work of both Goodwin and Owen on assurance, since for both, communion with the Son as the elder brother, and with the Spirit as the Spirit of adoption, are central means to achieving assurance of faith. This entire expansion does not necessarily conflict with Burgess, but as we will see, it provides a different emphasis.

Notwithstanding all this, the major impression one draws from the Savoy formulation is one of essential unity with the WCF. Where there are changes, they appear mainly as additions. They expand on the consensus of Westminster without fundamentally disrupting it. We can say confidently at this point that Goodwin (who we know already agreed to the Westminster formulation) and now Owen are in essential agreement with what the Westminster divines wrote (with almost no dissension) not ten years before.

Owen on Psalm 130

In 1668, Owen published an exposition on Psalm 130. If there was any hint of dissonance between the WCF formulations on assurance and Owen himself, those differences—if they existed in the first place—seem to have evaporated by the time of the publication of the these sermons.

For one thing, Owen in these sermons clearly affirms the distinction between saving faith and assurance, stating unequivocally, "There is or may be a saving persuasion or discovery of forgiveness in God, where there is no assurance of any particular interest therein."[38]

---

38. Owen, *Works*, 6:415.

In other words, one can be truly saved, having received the forgiveness of God in Christ, without assurance of having received it. Once again, our purpose is not to trace or explain the apparent changes in Owen's theology, but it is to show the clear codification of the Westminster consensus in the writings of Burgess's contemporaries in order to better understand Burgess himself.

Owen continues with this conviction. In the context of a slightly different argument, he writes:

> Let them [real believers] be asked whether they came so easily by their faith and apprehensions of forgiveness easily or no. 'Alas!' saith one, 'these twenty years have I been following after God, and yet I have not arrived unto an abiding a cheering persuasion of it.' 'I know what it cost me, what trials, difficulties, temptations I wrestled with, and went through withal, before I obtained it,' saith another. 'What I have attained unto hath been of unspeakable mercy; and it is my daily prayer that I may be preserved in it by the exceeding greatness of the power of God, for I continually wrestle with storms that are ready to drive me from my anchor.' A little of this discourse may be sufficient to convince poor, dark, carnal creatures of the folly and vanity of their confidence.[39]

If there can still be any doubt about Owen's mature position, this extended quote surely should suffice to disabuse us of it:

> Evangelical assurance is not a thing that consisteth in any point, and so incapable of variation. It may be higher or lower, greater or less, obscure or attended with more evidence. It is not quite lost when it is not quite at its highest. God sometimes marvelously raiseth the souls of his saints with some close and near approaches unto them, – gives them a sense of his eternal love, a taste of the embraces of his Son and the inhabitation of the Spirit, without the least intervening disturbance; and this is their assurance. But this life is not a season to be always taking wages in; our work is not yet done; we are not always to abide in this mount; we must down again into the battle, – fight again, cry again, complain again. Shall the soul be thought now to have lost its assurance? Not at all. It had before assurance with joy, triumph and exaltation; it hath now, or

---

39. Ibid., 6:508–9.

may have, with wrestling, cries, tears, and supplications. And a man's assurance may be as good, as true, when he lies on the earth with a sense of sin, as when he is carried up to the third heaven with a sense of love and foretaste of glory.[40]

Owen perhaps provides a way of reconciling this very clear affirmation of the Westminster doctrine with his earlier statements that seemed to point in another direction. In so doing, he also provides a helpful guide to understanding just what the divines may have meant when they described "infallible assurance." Owen's quote comes from his commentary on Hebrews, which, as we have noted, contains one of the major texts used to distinguish between types of assurance at Westminster, Heb. 6:11.[41] Owen writes:

> There is the πληροφορία of this hope, – the 'full assurance' of it. Hope hath its degrees, as faith has also. There is a *weak* or a *little* faith, and a strong or a great faith. So there is an imperfect and a more perfect hope. This 'full assurance' is not of the nature or essence of it, but an *especial degree* of it in its own improvement. A weak, imperfect hope, will give but weak and imperfect relief under trouble; but that which riseth up unto the full assurance will complete our relief. Wherefore, as hope itself is necessary, so is this degree of it, especially where trials do abound. Yet neither is hope in this degree absolute, or absolutely perfect. Our minds in this world are not capable of such a degree of assurance in spiritual things as to free us from assaults to the contrary, and impressions of fear sometimes from those assaults: but there is such a degree attainable as is always victorious; which will give the soul peace at all times, and sometimes fill it with joy.[42]

However, despite the basic agreement (at least at this date) between Owen and the Westminster consensus, it should also be noted that there was an expansion of the consensus in Owen. We see that Owen's emphases often differed from those of the WCF. For

40. Ibid., 6:551.
41. See chapter 4.
42. John Owen, *Epistle to the Hebrews*, 7 vols. (Edinburgh: Banner of Truth, 1991 repr.), 5:200.

instance, Owen recognized that the WCF statement left a great number of questions unanswered regarding the search for full assurance. Owen felt compelled to add his own instruction as to how one might receive the kind of assurance envisioned as a possibility in the WCF. He acknowledges that the effects of regeneration might serve as a kind of practical indicator of regeneration, a *syllogismus practicus* (practical syllogism), for gaining assurance of faith. He writes, "A due spiritual consideration of the causes and effects of regeneration is the ordinary way and means whereby the souls of believers come to be satisfied concerning the work of God in them and upon them."[43] He also writes a great deal about the need to wait. Since clear assurance often did not come immediately, it was necessary to patiently wait upon the Lord for it. But perhaps most importantly for our purposes, the following quote shows Owen's general attitude to the use of reasoning and syllogisms to arrive at a settled assurance:

> Waiting is the only way to an establishment of assurance; we cannot speed by haste; yea, nothing puts the end so far away as making too much haste. . . . And let not any think any think to make out their difficulties any other way: their own reasonings will not bring them to any establishing conclusion; for they may lay down propositions, and have no considerable objections to lie against either of them, and yet be far enough from that sweet consolation, joy, and assurance which is the product of the conclusion, when God is not pleased to give it in. Yea, a man may sometimes gather up consolation to himself upon such terms, but it will not abide.[44]

Although Owen here indicates once again his conclusions about assurance, reasoning will not bring an established conclusion in one's mind about salvation. It may bring consolation for a brief time, but it will not last. His major expansion on the Westminster doctrine

43. Owen, *Works*, 6:5.
44. Ibid., 6:553–55.

actually comes in his discussion of the ways in which the Holy Spirit bears immediate witness to the souls of believers, not through a syllogistic deduction, but through an immediate and internal work on the heart. This internal and immediate work may take time (which is why he enjoins patience); but one thing is clear: it is not attained primarily through the use of one's reasoning faculties.

Owen and Goodwin on the Sealing of the Spirit

Given this emphasis, it should come as no surprise that Owen's major contribution to the discussion of assurance after Westminster came in the area of pneumatology. Although his expositions of Psalm 130 give perhaps the most material on the assurance of faith, it is his work on the Holy Spirit where we see his most distinctive work on the topic. Specifically, his work on the sealing of the Spirit must be looked at in greater detail.

For the most part, Calvin and the other early Reformers saw the sealing of the Holy Spirit, as introduced in Eph. 1:13, to be a work of God synonymous with conversion. Calvin writes this on Eph. 1:13:

> But is it not the faith itself which is here said to be sealed by the Holy Spirit? If so, faith goes before the sealing. I answer, there are two operations of the Spirit in faith, corresponding to the two parts of which faith consists, as it enlightens, and as it establishes the mind. The commencement of faith is knowledge: the completion of it is a firm and steady conviction, which admits of no opposing doubt. Both, I have said, are the work of the Spirit. No wonder, then, if Paul should declare that the Ephesians, who received by faith the truth of the gospel, were confirmed in that faith by the seal of the Holy Spirit.[45]

We can see from this two important parts of Calvin's view. First, Calvin considers the sealing of the Holy Spirit to be something that

---

45. John Calvin, *Commentary on Ephesians* (AGES Bible Software), 17.

is part of true faith. Second, the sealing of the Spirit is a work directly connected with assurance. Both are notable for our understanding of Owen and Burgess.

Later this work of the Spirit in sealing was distinguished from a believer's consciousness of that work,[46] which led to the more thoroughgoing formulations of Richard Sibbes, who declared:

> Now, when the soul is thus convinced of the evil that is in us, and of the good that is in Christ, and with this convincing is inclined and moved by the Holy Spirit, as, indeed, the Holy Spirit doth all, then upon this the Spirit vouchsafeth a *superadded work*, – as the Spirit doth still add to his own work, – he added a confirming work, which is here called, 'sealing.' That seal is not faith, for the apostle saith, '*After* you believed, ye were sealed,' Eph i. 13. So that this sealing is not of the work of faith, but it is a work of the Spirit upon faith, assuring the soul of its estate in grace.[47]

Owen, like Calvin, identified the sealing of the Spirit as a gift of the Spirit given to individuals at the time of their conversion. This is significant because, as we will see, the sealing of the Spirit was one of the primary ways in which many of Owen's and Burgess's contemporaries (Goodwin is one) worked through the doctrine of assurance. Owen writes:

> It hath been generally conceived that this sealing with the Spirit is that which gives assurance unto believers – and so, indeed, it doth, although the way whereby it doth it hath not been rightly apprehended; and, therefore, none have been able to declare the especial nature of that act of the Spirit whereby he seals us, whence such assurance should ensue. . . . The Spirit himself . . . is the great evidence, the great ground of assurance, which we have that God hath taken us into a near and dear revelation unto himself, 'because he hath given us of his Spirit.'[48]

---

46. See Beeke, *Assurance of Faith*, 254.
47. Richard Sibbes, *Works of Richard Sibbes*, 7 vols. (Edinburgh: Banner of Truth, 1973 repr.), 3:455.
48. Owen, *Works*, 4:405.

Goodwin's view on the sealing of the Holy Spirit also has significant bearing on his own view of assurance. Like Owen, this comes out most clearly in his analysis of Eph. 1:13, but while Owen understands this text in much the same way as Calvin had before, Goodwin takes an entirely different approach. Interestingly, Goodwin assumes that the sealing ministry of the Holy Spirit is synonymous with an aware assurance. Because he does not believe that this kind of assurance is properly or necessarily associated with saving faith, he denies that sealing is something that happens immediately when one believes. In essence, Goodwin almost seems to work backward. He determines what sealing is (clear assurance of one's own interest in the death of Christ); then, since that is presumed to be distinct from saving faith, he can surmise that sealing and saving faith occur at distinct points in time.[49] In fact, Goodwin discusses the view of Calvin and others who took sealing to be synonymous in time with saving faith. His rejection is based on the fact that this would make assurance of one's salvation to be synonymous in time with saving faith, a possibility he rejects out of hand.[50]

Goodwin seems to hold out the sealing ministry of the Spirit as a second tier of Christian experience. Beeke has called Goodwin's perspective on sealing "beyond the pale of the 'typical' Christian. It is, as it were, a 'second-level' experience, producing almost as great a change in the believer's feelings as his initial conversion."[51] Indeed, this echoes Goodwin's own language. He writes, "It is a new conversion, it will make a man differ from himself in what he was before in that manner almost as conversion doth before he was converted. There is a new edition of all a man's graces,

---

49. Michael S. Horton, "Thomas Goodwin and the Puritan Doctrine of Assurance: Continuity and Discontinuity in the Reformed Tradition, 1600–1680" (PhD diss., University of Coventry, 1998), 289.
50. Ibid.
51. Beeke, *Assurance of Faith*, 339.

when the Holy Ghost comes as a sealer."[52] Horton summarizes this position: "Thus, as faith might lack assurance, so regeneration could lack sealing, and one can see how easily such an emphasis might lead to a greater focus on personal experience and the search for reaching a higher stage of Christian life that is not enjoyed by every believer."[53]

Goodwin and Owen on the Use of Syllogisms

Perhaps it should be clear at this point why the issue of the sealing of the Spirit was so significant to each of these men's understanding of the doctrine of assurance. It was more than simply a question of the exegesis of an isolated New Testament text; it was, rather, a critical pointer to the theological place in which one might put the doctrine of assurance. For Owen, assurance was not primarily found through the syllogisms but rather through the direct contemplation and appropriation of the work of the Triune God on one's behalf. For Goodwin, too, communion with the Triune God was the key, but he additionally referred to this in terms of the sealing of the Holy Spirit.

We would expect from this that Goodwin, like Owen, would have little time for the use of syllogisms. This is certainly borne out by Goodwin's writings. He begins by talking in terms of a "two-fold assurance":

> But now there is a twofold assurance of salvation, that we may yet go further in examining what is intended in it. . . . There is, first, an assurance by sense, by conditional promises, whereby a man, seeing the image of God upon his heart, to which promises are made, cometh comfortably to believe that he is in the estate of grace. But then, secondly, there is an immediate assurance of the Holy Ghost, by a heavenly and divine light, of a divine authority, which the Holy Ghost sheddeth in a man's heart (not having relation to grace wrought, or

---

52. Goodwin, *Works*, 1:251.
53. Horton, "Goodwin and Assurance," 291.

anything in a man's self,) whereby he sealeth him up to the day of redemption. And this is the great seal of all the rest. The one way is *discoursive*; a man gathereth that God loveth him from the effect, as we gather there is fire because there is smoke. But the other is *intuitive*, as the angels are said to know things. It is such a knowledge as whereby we know the whole is greater than the part, we do not stand discoursing. There is light that cometh and overpowereth a man's soul, and assureth him that God is his, and he is God's, and that God loveth him from everlasting.[54]

This division between "discoursive" and "intuitive" assurance is much the same as what we saw in Owen. Once again, it may provide for us some insight into the possible terminology of the WCF itself, which refers to "infallible" assurance. But beyond that, what we can see from Goodwin is that he does not consider these discursive means of assurance to be most useful or most to be sought after. He does see these as helpful, normative, and even perhaps part of the Spirit's own witness, but they are not the kind of ultimate assurance that he enjoins believers to seek after. The discursive witness (by which he means assurance via syllogism) can never provide full assurance.[55] Full assurance is "fetched out according to the records of God's own breast, and quoteth not, nor referreth us not to *any dealing of God with us, or work in us, but is an immediate voice of God's Spirit.*"[56] This is contrasted in Goodwin in that same sentence with "The testimony of both those is fetched and produced out of the records that are written in our own bosoms, from those gracious acts and dispositions, and dealings of God with our spirits, in drawing us to faith, and justifying, and also sanctifying us; and they are called our spirits."[57]

---

54. Goodwin, *Works*, 1:233 (italics in original).
55. For a fuller discussion of the way in which Goodwin acknowledges the Spirit's work through these discursive means yet ultimately encourages believers to move beyond them, see Beeke, *Assurance*, 336–38.
56. Goodwin, *Works*, 8:363 (italics mine).
57. Ibid., 8:362–63.

Similarly, we recall the words of Owen, who wrote in part, "Their own reasonings will not bring them to any establishing conclusion; for they may lay down propositions. . . . Yea, a man may sometimes gather up consolation to himself upon such terms, but it will not abide."[58]

Owen and Goodwin and the Westminster Consensus: Conclusions

John Owen did not write a treatise on assurance, but his catechisms, commentaries, and work on the Savoy Declaration did afford him the opportunity to write a good deal on the topic. His writing after the WCF seems to follow along the same lines as the WCF itself, but several things are notable. First, a large part of Owen's writing on the topic relates to broader questions of pneumatology. This pneumatological emphasis is something we see in Owen and Goodwin, although it is notably absent from the statements contained in the confession itself. We also do not see this expansion on the WCF found so prominently in Burgess. Also, we see in Owen (and Goodwin) that an understanding of how assurance functions is directly connected with his discussions of communion with the Triune God. As such, his writing on assurance is focused quite squarely on the question of how one can have an immediate and full assurance based not on syllogistic reasoning, but on our apprehension of God himself. In so doing, he does not employ the language of sealing to describe what this assurance consists of. In fact, his understanding of this is the same as Calvin's in that he sees sealing as part of the act of God in conversion. But nonetheless, Owen is concerned with direct knowledge of one's interest in God's saving

---

58. Ibid., 6:553–55.

work, and his attention to this indicates the necessity of a clearer explanation that went beyond the consensus reached at Westminster.

Goodwin, too, faced a pastoral situation that demanded clearer answers to many of the questions that the WCF left open. To be sure, Goodwin was certain of some things that clearly are affirmed by the WCF. Like the WCF itself—indeed, perhaps more fully than the WCF itself—Goodwin made clear that the kind of assurance described by the WCF (an inward full persuasion that one is absolutely in possession of salvation) is not an essential component of saving faith. He uses several proofs to advance this notion, including the facts that the publican, who was justified rather than the Pharisee, was not specifically said to be assured of that; similarly, Abraham, though a believer credited with God's righteousness, was never said to *know* that God had done such a work; finally, he concludes that since believers can commit gross sins, then gross doubt is also a possibility.[59] Goodwin writes that his task is:

> to keep such as have their hearts drawn to Christ and upheld to believe, though without such prevailing assurance, from such discouraging thoughts, as therefore to think their estates accursed, and that they cannot be in the estate of grace, because they want such a work. And also my end is to keepf off those that have assurance superadded to faith, from censuring the present condition of many of their brethren, as if they were without grace, because they want such assurance. . . . If blessedness then lies herein, then surely the estate of those persons was such as their sins were forgiven, and yet they wanted assurance.[60]

For Goodwin (as with Owen), assurance was first of all something that also involved communion with the triune God. He writes:

> [As in believing,] . . . so it is in assurance: sometimes a man's communion and converse is with the one, sometimes with the other; sometimes with the Father, then with the Son, and then with the Holy

---

59. Horton, "Goodwin and Assurance," 259.
60. Goodwin, *Works*, 8:339.

Ghost; sometimes his heart is drawn out to consider the Father's love in choosing, and then the love of Christ in redeeming, and so the love of the Holy Ghost, that searcheth the deep things of God, and revealeth them to us, and taketh all the pains with us; and so a man goes from one witness to another distinctly, which, I say, is the communion that John would have us to have.[61]

In expanding upon the silences of the WCF, Goodwin employed the language of the sealing of the Spirit; in fact, the Spirit's sealing work became synonymous with this second work in the believer's life. Goodwin, too, placed less emphasis on the use of syllogisms, which he referred to as "discursive" means of assurance. Like Owen, his attention to these matters indicates a strong pastoral need for clearer instruction on the important matter of assurance. While Westminster provided the framework and highlighted the importance of the question, it was left to others to further expand upon it. Perhaps Goodwin's view (which became a dominant view hereafter) could be summed up with this extended quote. He writes on the witness of the Spirit in assurance:

And this witness is immediate, that is, it builds not his testimony on anything in us; it is not a testimony fetched out of a man's self, or the work of the Spirit in man, as the others were; for the Spirit speaks not by his effects, but speaks from himself, and confirms the other, and therefore is said to witness with the other, that is, comes in to strengthen their witness. And though the Holy Ghost joined with water and blood in their testimony (for grace without him cannot evidence, as it cannot work without him), yet so his testimony lay hid in theirs, as they are said to witness, and his testimony is concealed though he allegeth them, and clears them up to a man, and therefore a man shall find the same signs sometimes evidence to him, and sometimes not, as the Spirit irradiates them; and yet this testimony of his is over and above theirs, and severed from theirs, and therefore is said to make a third witness, which as witnessing in the other he could not be said to be. But though this testimony of the Spirit be beyond the witness of faith or water, and

---

61. Ibid., 8:378–79.

above what the word in any sound or syllables carries with it, yet it is always according to it, and therefore they are said to be 'sealed with the Spirit of promise,' Eph. 1:13. It calls up some word that echoes to it, and goes with it. The Spirit opens God's mind in some words, and also, though it may come in from an evidence received and entertained from the former witnesses, blood and water, and therefore is said to witness with the other, as coming to back what they said, yet so as their testimony then comes to be considered but as the occasion upon which this of the Spirit is let in, and as the hint given; but it raiseth the soul up higher, and the other testimony as it were falls down, and God's immediate mind and acception out of the riches of his grace, entertains a man's soul and thoughts. For as Christ received no testimony from man, though he says John gave testimony . . . . And this witness, though it is placed first (after the manner of the Hebrews and other Scriptures), yet comes in as the last of the three, as being the greatest, and that which puts all out of question, which the other did not so fully; and therefore he is said to witness with our spirits, because their testimony is usually given in first; this of the Spirit backs and confirms what they said, as seals come in after a man's hand is set.[62]

Conclusion

Notwithstanding their differences, Owen and Goodwin had a remarkably similar approach to filling in the gaps left by the consensus at Westminster. They both understood that more needed to be said; their pastoral circumstances made this imperative. They also both primarily focused their energy in moving their readers to an embrace of a direct assurance from the Holy Spirit, something that came neither at the moment of conversion, nor through the use of discursive, reasoned, or syllogistic means of attaining it. This stands in direct contrast to Burgess. In seeking to explain assurance, Burgess draws mostly upon the types of proofs that Goodwin might have referred to as "discursive." Goodwin and Owen dismiss the idea that

---

62. Goodwin, *Works*, 8:366–67.

a Christian should *merely* rest on the promises of the word or look to the fruit of one's own life. Something more is needed.

For both Goodwin and Owen, assurance is immediate and mystical, and ultimately Trinitarian in its focus. It is to be sought by all believers, though it might be received at differing times by only some. While Burgess is thoroughly Trinitarian, his Trinitarianism does not manifest itself in the type of instructions on assurance given by Goodwin and Owen. So, to return to Beeke's summary of Puritan assurance quoted at the end of the previous chapter, it would seem that his discussion does not go far enough in articulating the differences between these post-Westminster Puritan theologians.

5

The Danger of False Assurance

Frameworks after Westminster

As we have seen already, one of the challenges facing those who followed the formulation of the Westminster Confession of Faith (WCF) was that, while the WCF gave a framework for understanding certain possibilities—true assurance, false assurance, lack of assurance—it did not define clearly how each of these possibilities was to be identified in an individual. While the "regular means" are proposed for the acquiring of true assurance, there is no comparable suggestion made for evaluating counterfeit or presumptuous claims of assurance.

This is a pastoral problem for at least two reasons. First, it is a genuine problem when addressing some who may want to come to a full assurance of their faith. These earnestly concerned individuals would need to know what kind of evidence accurately serves as proof. Second, the pastor who agreed with the WCF framework would also need to determine how to evaluate the claims of someone who might state that he had received some kind of absolute assurance of faith. The WCF, aiming as it was at defining the options within an individual believer's life, did not provide a framework for evaluating such claims.

In addition, while the WCF allowed for the possibility of true assurance, it also indicated that believers might not possess assurance of their salvation—that, in fact, assurance could be a back-and-forth phenomenon. The WCF makes clear this possibility when it asserts, "True believers may have the assurance of their salvation divers ways shaken, diminished, and intermitted; as, by negligence in preserving of it, by falling into some special sin which wounds the conscience and grieves the Spirit; by some sudden or vehement temptation, by God's withdrawing the light of His countenance, and suffering even such as fear Him to walk in darkness and to have no light."[1] Yet as with the other statements of the confession, this one is not filled out in great detail, and it would be left to others such as Anthony Burgess to expand it in ways that would fit with the pastoral situations faced by the pastors in the Westminster tradition.

One of the great challenges Burgess, Goodwin, and Owen must have faced, if their writings are any indication, was that of the genuinely converted person who nonetheless was plagued with doubt. This is perhaps the overarching reason that they wrote so much on the topic of assurance.

False Assurance

The possibility of false assurance is one that each writer (but Burgess especially) considers to be a strong one. Burgess recognized that there might be aspects of someone's life that could, from one angle, be

1. Westminster Confession of Faith 18.4.

considered signs of true grace but are in fact no signs at all. In his first treatise on assurance, he spends at least sixteen chapters specifically addressing things that might normally be seen as evidences of saving faith but, according to him, should not be used as signs of assurance. These topics include "Church-priviledges"; "Gifts and Parts in matters of Religion"; "affections and sweet motions of heart in holy things"; "Judgements, Opinions and Disputes"; "the greatest sufferings for Christ"; "Zeal and diligence in false Worship"; "External obedience to the Law of God"; "Divine faith or perswasion of the truths in Religion"; "every peacable frame of heart, and perswasion of Gods love"; "outward successe, prosperity and greatnesse in the world"; and "a mans leaving those grosse sins he hath lived in."[2] These are given in addition to chapters that treat the topic more generally, with titles such as "Laying open the Counterfeits of the New-Birth."[3] Add to this the fact that the second volume of *Spiritual Refining* is entirely made up of a treatment of sin and its blinding effects, with a special emphasis on hypocrisy and religious formality.[4]

Each of these must be examined in further detail, but Burgess's treatment of the topic does not end with simply diagnosing the possibility of such a presumptuous state. He also expounds quite

2. Anthony Burgess, *Spiritual Refining, Spiritual Refining, or, a Treatise of Grace and Assurance Part I: Wherein Are Handled, the Doctrine of Assurance, the Use of Signs in Self-Examination, How True Graces May Be Distinguished from Counterfeit, Several True Signs of Grace, and Many False Ones, the Nature of Grace, under Divers Scripture-Notions or Titles, as Regeneration, the New-Creature, the Heart of Flesh, Vocation, Sanctification, &C.: Many Chief Questions (Occasionally) Controverted between the Orthodox and the Arminians: As Also Many Cases of Conscience, Tending to Comfort and Confirm Saints, [and] Undeceive and Convert Sinners*. (London: Printed by Jo. Streater, for T.U., and are to be sold by Thomas Johnson, 1658). Items taken from section entitled "The Contents."

3. Ibid.

4. Anthony Burgess, *Spiritual Refining Part II or, a Treatise of Sinne with its Causes, Differences, Mitigations and Aggravations, Particularly of the desparate* Deceitfulnes of Mans Heart, *of* Presumptuous *and* Reigning Sins, *and of* Hypocrisie *and* Formalitie *in Religion* (London: Thomas Newberry, 1654).

comprehensively on the evidences that would point to a false, rather than true assurance—or, to use Burgess's own language, to discern evidences that would distinguish that which is mere presumption from that which is true assurance.

Burgess acknowledges that the major difference between presumption and genuine assurance lies in their respective roots. Whereas genuine assurance is rooted in the testimony of God the Holy Spirit, presumption is rooted in sinful pride.[5] True to form, however, Burgess does not dwell at great length on this internal condition. He always seems more concerned with that which can be observed and marshaled as objective evidence. Instead, he attempts to denote the marks that serve as evidence of an individual's status before God.

In describing the individual whose testimony of assurance is nothing more than presumption, Burgess begins by citing the significance of the attitude one has to the law of God. He notes that the apostle Paul, describing his own state in Romans 7, is seemingly undone by the law, feeling quite condemned in the light of its standard of holiness.[6] In contrast, Burgess notes that presumptuous people have little regard for God's law, or at a minimum, they fail to feel its full weight upon their sinful hearts. Another way of putting this would be to say that true believers, accurately assured of their salvation, would see themselves as sinners in the sight of God. Burgess writes, "So that the presumption of unregenerate men ariseth from the stupidity and blindnesse in them; whereas the godly Assurance is wrought out of a gracious Illumination about the height, depth and breadth of sinne, with a tender affection about the weight and burden of it. Art thou then one who presumes of the love of God, and restest in the goodness of thy heart?"[7]

5. Burgess, *Spiritual Refining*, 27.
6. Ibid.

This is essentially an internal marker, and it is connected in Burgess's treatise with what he sees as the root of true assurance. But it is also a marker that one could use pastorally in a diagnostic fashion. Assuming that individuals were honest about their attitude toward the law or feelings about their own sinful state, Burgess was offering a clear diagnostic tool to separate true assurance from false assurance. That is, even when describing an essentially internal marker, he begins doing so in a way that gives objective evidence for analysis and conclusions.

He does, however continue with the internal roots, stating that the motivation for seeking and receiving true assurance would be different from that which drives presumption; in addition, he does note that each of these has different spiritual roots.[8] Deep humiliation over the extent of sin is the primary attitude that characterizes a true assurance; presumption about salvation is marked by a presumptuous attitude toward sin in general. But again, what is remarkable about his discourse on true assurance and presumption is the extent to which he relies upon external markers to give evidence of presumption.

At this point, we see Burgess build directly on the legacy of the WCF statement on assurance. One of the ways in which the WCF advocates fostering assurance is through the use of ordinary means. Burgess builds upon this idea and applies it to the evaluation of whether someone has a genuine or a false assurance of faith. He believes that one way of definitively determining the truthfulness of someone's assurance is through examining whether or not the person makes use of the ordinary means of spiritual growth and grace. His simple slogan is "So that where Diligence, and all Diligence is not used, there is no Assurance."[9] Once again, a pastor who is trying to

---

7. Ibid.
8. Ibid., 28.

discern whether someone's claim to assurance is real or presumptuous can look to the person's diligence. If someone is diligent in the pursuit of holiness and in the use of the ordinary means, then one can have greater certainty about the truthfulness of that person's claim to assurance, since assurance itself is fostered by the ordinary means. To explain further what he means by this, Burgess writes,

> In earnest Prayer, holy use of Sacraments, walking universally in all Gods ways, is this godly certainty maintained; whereas carnal confidence is big, and swelling even in the neglect, yea prophane contempt of the means. A man that doth not pray, that polluteth himself with daily sins, yet he is thoroughly perswaded of his happiness. As therefore in the ordinary passages of Gods Providence, he is rightly judged a presume who will perswade himself of life, when yet he will neither eat or drink, be assured of wealth and riches, when yet he will use no Diligence: such an arrogant sottishness [stupification; excessive drunkenness, JLM] is in a spiritual presumer.[10]

The ordinary means of which the WCF speaks refer, for Burgess, to prayer and the right use of the sacraments, and in addition, to the general struggle against daily sin. Although the WCF itself does not outline the ordinary means in detail, it does list them in the catechism. Question 88 reads, "Q: What are the outward means whereby Christ communicateth to us the benefits of redemption? A: The outward and ordinary means whereby Christ communicateth to us the benefits of redemption, are his ordinances, especially the word, sacraments, and prayer; all which are made effectual to the elect for salvation."[11]

In addition, true assurance will persevere in the midst of difficulty and will cause one to hate sin more. While a presumptive attitude leads to greater pride and a corresponding lack of concern for sin, real

9. Ibid., 30.
10. Ibid.
11. Westminster Shorter Catechism, question 88. Taken from http://www.opc.org/sc.html. Accessed March 1, 2015.

assurance does the opposite. Real assurance makes one resist sin and the world even more, to think of it with far less affection than before; in fact, it will cause its bearer to hate sin even more. Burgess writes, "Consider therefore how thy Assurance worketh in thee, doth it put out all love to sin and the world? Doth it kill inordinate affections to things below, and raise up thy heart to God, delighting and rejoicing in him? This is a comfortable demonstration of good Assurance."[12]

The presence of this increasing affection in the heart for God and appreciation of God's nature and works over that which is earthly and sinful also keeps the discouragement of difficult circumstances from overcoming the believer. It does this by enflaming the heart of an individual with the love of God. So powerful is this love from God that the individual can never be completely distraught about circumstances again: he or she will persevere in the midst of them. In fact, Burgess argues that it is impossible to envision any kind of long-term perseverance in the midst of trials apart from such assurance:

This Certainty of our Propriety and Interest in God, is an Ark to the soul in the midst of many waters; whereas take any carnal confident man, his heart becomes like a stone within him, when all carnal hopes fail. And this is a precious symptom, see in the midst of these confusions thou livest in, when Heaven and Earth become mingled together. What makes thee rejoice and to lift up thy head with gladness? Is it that Knowledge thou hast of God to be thy God? Is it those pledges and pawns in thy soul of his eternal love and goodness unto thee? This is something. But alas, as the hypocrites joy, so his confidence will quickly perish. It is not a Star fixed in the Orb made of quintessential matter, but a blazing Star composed of flimsy materials, which will quickly consume and vanish away.[13]

We can see here once again the pattern of Burgess's writing in this area. He gives a clear test by which one can deduce the truthfulness

---

12. Burgess, *Spiritual Refining*, 30.
13. Ibid.

of a claim to assurance. In this case, the question is, Does it give joy in the midst of difficulties? He views difficulties as the way of testing the truthfulness of one's own claim to assurance, and also the way in which one might look at someone else's life and evaluate that person's claim. If the joy and confidence of an individual fades when trouble comes, then anyone evaluating the person's claim of assurance can discount it as presumption. Burgess seems interested in making the objective features of assurance clear. One is supposed to reason backward from these objective evidences to the truth or falsehood of the claim itself. In short, once again we see that the marks of true assurance—the evidences that can be used to deduce the reliability of someone's claim to have certainty of salvation—are, in Burgess's thinking, primarily external, observable by an individual and by those exercising pastoral care over the individual. In fact, Burgess's treatise makes the pastoral office central to the issue of discerning false assurance and reigniting the flame of assurance in those who have lost it. In fact, without understanding Burgess's view of the pastoral office and the ministry of preaching, we will not fully understand his notions of how to address false assurance.

False Assurance and the Role of Preaching

One of the most noticeable features of Burgess's expansions on the statements in the WCF on assurance comes in his discussion of the role of the minister and of the church in fostering assurance and in separating that which is true assurance from that which is false or presumptuous. For Burgess, the ministry of preaching plays a primary role in this kind of discernment about assurance. Burgess writes this on the subject:

> What the Heretick is in matter of Doctrine, the same is a carnal
> presumer in matter of practice and conversation. Now as the former

is seldom reduced, because there is obstinancy and contumacy in him against all admonitions; so is the latter scarce ever truly debased and humbled, because of self-love that cleaveth to him. But if ever any thing be able to overrule and conquer him, these remedies following are likely to do it. First, *A powerfull and soul-searching Ministry, that will so pierce into, and discover the hidden things of the heart, that thereby he may come to made known to himself.* The Ministry of the Word is like the Sunne in the firmament, from whose light nothing is hidden. Thus the Prophets, the Apostles, they were lights. And what conviction might the Jews have had of all their self-fullness and hypocrisies, if they had not shut their eyes against the light.[14]

Once again, we note not only that Burgess is emphasizing preaching (which he sure is), but also that he is trying to give careful and concrete methods for analysis of one's own heart or that of another. As we have noted this overall approach in the past, it is no surprise to find it here again. However, before we move on with this broader analysis, we must first consider briefly Burgess's overall view of preaching, since preaching quite obviously plays a major role in his reflection on the topic of false assurance.

We can begin this analysis of the connection between preaching and discerning false assurance by returning to Burgess's simple statement cited earlier about the *"diligent"* use of ordinary means being significant in maintaining assurance. Although in that statement and its immediate context, Burgess omits preaching as a part of the ordinary means of which one must diligently avail oneself, we must understand that for Burgess, preaching, perhaps more than anything else, was the means by which God separates true assurance from presumption. In fact, at one point, he calls it the *only* ordinary means:

The Ministry is the only ordinary way that God hath appointed, either for the beginnings or increase of grace. For the beginnings, Thus *Faith* is

14. Ibid., 32.

said *to come by hearing*, Rom 10:17. *And God hath begotten by his Word*, Jam. 1.18. And for the increase, *Eph.* 4. You may there see it is for the compleating of us in *a full stature of Christ.* Thus as the ordinary way of a mans life is by outward food and sustenance; so the ordinary meanes of all spiritual life is by the Ministry of the Word. Indeed some propound particular cases, as of Infants who do not hear, or of deaf men, or of some persons by unexpected calamities [illegible, possibly 'can'] where no Ministry is to be had; but we do not now speak of extraordinary wayes, we know God did feed the *Israelites* with *Manna* from heaven when they could have no ordinary food; but in Gods ordinary way, unless thou expect a miracle, the Ministry is the instrumental publique means.[15]

So for Burgess, the means of grace that God uses both to effect assurance and to distinguish between false presumption and true assurance is principally the preaching of the word. Where the WCF was silent (though it acknowledged the role of "ordinary means" in assurance), Burgess is emphatic. The public means that contributes most to a real assurance and that best divides between true and false expressions of this is the preaching of God's word. Because of the connection in Burgess between preaching and assurance, we must turn to his discussion of preaching and its role more generally.

Burgess's sermon on John 17:6 clearly states Burgess's case with regard to preaching. He writes, "*That the end of the Ministry and Ministers should be to bring people to the knowledge of God, to the saving knowledge of Christ.*"[16] This, upon first reading, might seem to be simply the barest form of evangelism. But Burgess is not saying that the minister's work is identical to that of the evangelist. In fact, his

---

15. Burgess, *The Scripture Directory for Church-Officers and People, or, a Practical Commentary Upon the Whole Third Chapter of the First Epistle of St. Paul to the Corinthians to Which Is Annexed the Godly and the Natural Mans Choice, Upon Psal. 4, Vers. 6, 7, 8.* (London: Printed by Abraham Miller for T.U. and are to be sold by Thomas Underhill, George Calvert, and Henry Fletcher, 1659), 69.

16. Anthony Burgess, *Expository Sermons Upon the Whole 17th Chapter of the Gospel According to St John: or, Christ's Prayer Before his Passion Explicated, and both Practically and Polemically Improved* (London: Thomas Underhill, 1656), 166.

definition of what it means to bring people to a saving knowledge of Christ is that they dutifully preach "*all the Counsell of God.*"[17]

In fact, according to Burgess, this end is so important that the minster must not proclaim anything else. To mix proclamation of God's word with anything else is dangerous: "It's therefore a dangerous thing for a Minister of Christ to propound any other end principally at least but what is the end of the Ministry."[18]

The reason for this emphasis on biblical preaching was that it was Burgess's larger conviction that the purpose of the preacher's work really was to effect change, guiding the souls of his hearers to a saving knowledge of Jesus Christ. He was to point his congregation *effectually* to Christ. Union with Christ was at the end of it all. He writes this about the faithful preacher: "He doth not espouse people to himself, but to Christ; he wooeth and entreateth them for Christ: it is not your good to us, but your obedience unto Christ, that we aime at."[19]

Burgess supports this contention with quotations from the Scriptures themselves, not merely to illustrate, but to prove the doctrine. In this case, the relevant example is John the Baptist:

> Thus *John Baptist* calls himself *the friend of the Bridegroom*, John 3.29 which is the duty of every Minister; the friend of the Bridegroom, which standeth and heareth, rejoiceth greatly because of the Bridegrooms voice. It's an allusion to the custome in those dayes; the Bridegroom he had his friend and spokesman to bring him into the Brides presence, and he heard their conference; if there were a willing agreement between them concluded, then the friend rejoiced greatly. Thus it was with *John*, and also with every Minister: We are Christs spokesman, we wooe you, we entreat you, we bring you and Christ together every Sabbath day. Bow if any soul will receive him, and be married to him, forsaking his former lusts, and all by-past sinnes, then is the friend of the Bridegrooms

17. Burgess, *Scripture Directory*, 166.
18. Ibid., 167.
19. Ibid., 63.

joy greatly fulfilled; it would therefore be horrible unfaithfulness in us, if we should do as *Sampson's* friend did to him, who got *Sampson's* wife for himself.[20]

So the preacher has—not only as his aim, but also as his measure of success—the marrying of a soul to Jesus Christ.

As the following quote will show, this definition of successful preaching has significant implications in Burgess's estimation for the individual discerning true and false assurance:

> Hath the Ministry been usefull to bring you effectually to Christ himself? This is what *Paul* desired. You may hear much, you may pray much, you may be much affected with the matter preached, and yet all this while not close with Christ; to receive him as a Savior, and to obey him as a Lord. A woman may have many Letters and Tokens of love from him whom she loveth, and be much affected to him, yet not married to him, *nor enjoy him as her Husband*: And so, thou maist have some affections and good desires, but thou art not yet united to Christ. The work of the Ministry is not done, till we can leave you in the arms of Christ: Till we have prepared the way to lodge in your souls.[21]

Note that Burgess is looking not only to the conversion of individuals to Christ, but to their enjoyment of the marriage with Christ. He envisions preaching being the instrument of bringing to their consciousness the enjoyment of Christ's benefits for those who believe. This would surely at least entail an assurance that one really was wedded to Christ; preaching was intended to foster this. Of course, it does not function *ex opere operato* for the congregant. In fact, Burgess writes this: "Experience witnesseth, that after ten thousand Sermons, men remain as ignorant, and as bruteth as before. The words reach only to the ear, but they make no forcible impression upon the soul. So then, the Ministry doth not beget grace, as the fire burneth, or the hatchet cutteth; which are Instruments

20. Ibid.
21. Ibid., 66 (italics mine).

that work by their own inward disposition and power to produce their effects."[22] Burgess acknowledges that the ministry does not work everywhere. He contrasts this with fire, which under normal conditions burns in every location. Its effects are repeatable, but the effects of preaching are not.

Burgess further expounds on this measure of the preacher's success. He writes of the twofold end of preaching. Preaching can lead either to "a *corrupt, sinfull end*, or a *gracious, godly, plain and upright end.*" This aim of an upright end and the success of seeing it provide earthly comfort for the minister. He writes, "Oh this is a precious cordial, when under all the censures, reproaches, and uncharitableness of the world to the Ministry, Ministers can upon good grounds comfort themselves, that they have walked in all godly sincerity, endeavouring the salvation of mens soules, and with tender bowels mourning for those that go astray, rejoicing to see any person or families owning Christ, setting up his wayes and Ordinances."[23]

But the congregation, too, bears a responsibility in this matter. They ought to come to their Sunday service prepared to repent, to be illumined about their present state by the words of the preacher. They are to go ready to be informed, to have their former ignorance and disobedience reversed. Burgess even suggests questions for people to ask as they approach the service: "To what end am I going to the publike Assembly? Why go I to hear the Word preached? If I do not attain to the end I lose my labour; Is it not the end of preaching and the end of hearing to deliver me from my former ignorance, my former lusts; how then comes it about that I am still as I was?"[24] The burden for applying the word lay upon both preacher and hearer.

22. Ibid., 67.
23. Ibid., 63.
24. Ibid., 167.

However, if the hearers did not repent as a result of what they heard, if there was no change, then the blame lay with them.

Applied to the question of assurance, this means at least two things. First, since Burgess believed that the ultimate aim of preaching was to bring a soul in direct marital union with Christ, experiencing all the benefits therein, then preaching, for him, presented the best of the ordinary means for gaining or regaining assurance. But more to the point, Burgess also saw preaching as the means by which individuals become acutely attuned to the evidences that might prove their presumption with regard to assurance. To sit under a faithful preaching ministry meant that one was sitting under a ministry of conviction, a ministry that confronted them with truth and exposed their own error. For one engaged in the deductive spiritual process that Burgess's treatises demand, preaching is the essential component of revealing presumption.

Aside from the general application of Burgess's view of preaching to the question of false assurance, Burgess gives three specific reasons why preaching provides this essential component in exposing false assurance. First, preaching—especially preaching the law of God—exposes one's sin and shows it in the light of God's holiness.[25] He gives many examples of this type of preaching of the law and its effectiveness in exposing sin and presumption, but perhaps they could be summarized by his closing quote on the matter: 'Hence it is that men, to keep themselves from appearing as deformed as they are, limit the sense of the law, as if it were not so exact as it is, like the Elephant Demudding the water that it may not see its own deformity.'[26] The clear and pristine preaching of God's law exposes the evidence for presumption in the clearest way possible; from this

---

25. Burgess, *Spiritual Refining*, 33.
26. Ibid., 33. "Demudding" is an archaic word not in usage today. It means muddying. Compounding the archaism is the problem that the word is slightly obscured in the manuscript to which I have access. Nonetheless, I am fairly confident in transcribing it the way I have here.

unsullied exposure of the evidence, one cannot help but deduce the correct conclusion about the veracity of one's claim to assurance.

It is not just the preaching of the law that invariably exposes the veracity of one's claim to assurance; it is also the preaching of Christ. In this case, Burgess has in mind particularly the preaching of Christ's righteousness being the only hope for sinners.[27] What Burgess assumes is that in hearing a clear proclamation of the glory of Christ's imputed righteousness to the believer, those whose claims of assurance are presumptuous will be forced into confronting the falsehood of their confession. Their lack of appreciation for the glories of Christ, and their lack of understanding about what all this means for their salvation, will provide for them clear evidence in deducing the veracity of their claims. It may, in Burgess's estimation, also provide the same kind of evidence for evaluating someone else's claim to assurance: in seeing how another individual responds to the revelation of Christ's glory, one can infer the degree to which they are truly converted and reliably certain of their own saving faith.

The third specific reason for the primacy of the preached word in exposing presumption is that listening to the preached word in a state of self-denial or self-deception brings a host of trials and difficulties into the life of the hearer. This somewhat surprising contention in Burgess's treatise nonetheless fits his basic pattern. He is looking for the things that will reveal clear evidence one way or another about assurance. Upon confronting the clear evidence, the individual must then reason backward, deducing from the clear evidence the actual status of his or her heart. In this case, the evidence that will be given from the stimulus of preaching is the evidence of unrest and affliction. The preached word, Burgess argues, operates like "a sword in our bowels."[28] Again, he writes of preaching, "For when God shall thus

27. Ibid.
28. Ibid.

by his Word thunder in our ears and hearts; When he shall also outwardly scourge & afflict, then is a man many times taken off from his lofty imaginations."[29] The afflictions, in Burgess's thinking, are a result of the thundering sword of the word to the bowels. The preached word, in some fashion, is said to bring with it strife and unease to such an extent that it will disabuse any false professions of assurance, once again providing clear evidence for the presumptuous to see their falsehood clearly.

The Evidentiary Approach to Assurance and Its Dangers

In expanding on the consensus of the WCF in the area of false assurance, Burgess consistently attempts to find ways to determine clear, objective evidence. This is in keeping with his pattern of *attaining* assurance as well. In both attaining assurance and deducing the veracity of a claim to assurance, Burgess operates deductively. In fact, he spends a great deal of his time in the treatise arguing that this is the appropriate way forward. He goes so far as to say:

> If a Christian may not gather the grace of Justification and Sanctification, by the fruits thereof, it would be for one of these grounds, either first the impossibility of it, as the Papists urge, it would not be possible for a man to know when grace is in him: but that is false, for howsoever a mans heart is naturally deceitfull, yet when regenerated, God takes away that guile in it, and so farre as it is spiritual it is sincere and cannot lie; Or secondly, This would be uselesse, having Assurance by Gods Spirit, what needs evidences by inherent graces; This is to light a candle when the Sunne shineth; but the testimony of the Spirit, and the evidence of graces make up one compleat witnesse, and therefore are not to be disjoined, much less opposed, as is further to be cleared. . . . Holiness of life must be joined to abilities of the head. . . . As many good and holy actions thou dost, so many rings though hast upon thy hand; These adorn thee more than gold or silver.[30]

29. Ibid.

As was the case with receiving assurance, so it is in the case of assessing the truthfulness of one's claim to assurance. To that end, we have also seen that the primary means of producing appropriate evidence is the preaching of the word. But the evidence to be used in deduction (distinguished here from that which produces or displays the evidence) is varied. We see in Burgess's treatise a kind of taxonomy of evidence to be used in deducing one's spiritual condition. But along with this taxonomy of evidence, Burgess also provides warnings in pursuing the evidentiary approach for which he so clearly advocates.

Burgess, while strongly affirming that good works are an important and necessary evidence for discerning between true and false assurance, nonetheless provides several warnings about taking this approach. It is clear that he understands the potential pitfalls inherent in looking at signs to judge assurance. He writes, "The work that remaineth at this time, is to advertise you against those many rocks you may split at, while you proceed by signs; for although this method (as you have heard) be lawfull, and a duty, yet there is required much art and skill to manage this work, insomuch that herein he ought to have had his senses exercised to discern between good and evil."[31]

Burgess's first warning in this regard is that there is no infallible sign that will absolutely show the veracity or presumption behind anyone's claim to assurance.[32] While many may seek after such a perfect sign, in Burgess's estimation, such a sign does not exist.

In fact, what Burgess is arguing here goes somewhat deeper. Not only does he understand that there no perfect sign by which someone can prove with absolute certainty the reliability of his or her

---

30. Ibid., 47–48.
31. Ibid., 55.
32. Ibid.

assurance, but he also uses this point to make a larger point about the nature of one's spiritual life. He reminds his readers that, although it is common practice for ministers of the gospel to point people toward self-examination and signs of real assurance, these are always presented as perfected graces in the believer's life, whereas often the signs true assurance come in an imperfect form.[33] Burgess even cautions against withholding judgment on the signs until one can see their final outcome. This is a key difference, as we will see, between his approach and that of Thomas Goodwin. Burgess writes that it is a mistake to consider temporary signs insufficient. They are in error who, "*When they approach no Sign sufficient, unlesse they have had an actual perseverance to the end.*"[34] Since this is a distinctive feature of Burgess's writing on the topic of false assurance, it is worth quoting what he has to say at length:

> Now although it be true, that the good ground differed from the bad, in that it held out to the end, yet that was not the only, nor the principal difference, but this perseverance was an effect flowing from the nature of the good soul. Although therefore afflictions and persecutions do detect the falseness of many, as appeareth *Matth 13.* yet it doth not follow, that therefore none can have Assurance, but such who are come to their journies end. The *Arminians* indeed much presse this, and therefore they hold, *There is no absolute and peremtory Election, but upon perseverance in faith and obedience.* Hence they joy in that with the Poet, *Ante obitum,* No man is happy before his death, because they may decline and apostatize from what they had. It cannot be denied but the revolt and degradation of those who have seemed pillars in the Church of God, hath much affrighted the godly, making them also fear, as if one day or another, In one temptation or other they should fall away: but they are to consider, That wheresoever grace is already truly wrought in a man's heart, there God hath made a promise to keep us until the end, so that we may be assured of perseverance as well as our present righteousness, for *God who beginneth a good work in us, Will also make an*

33. Ibid.
34. Ibid., 58.

end; and we have a gracious promise of God's care to us in the Prophet *Isaiah, That as he gave us being at first, and bore us in his arms, so he will also carry us on to old age itself,* as Gods grace hath planted, so he will water it, and give encrease to it.[35]

Later in the treatise, he gives another, somewhat related caveat: the signs themselves, while important, are never to be the objects of comfort in one's life. Only Christ should hold this position.[36] So for Burgess, signs may be found in an imperfect form, though they are often spoken of in their perfect form, and signs, while vital, are never truly the cause of hope.[37] Ultimately he writes:

> Without diligent scrutiny, we shall always be strangers to what is in our own souls. Thus many deceive their own souls, saying, They do repent, they do believe, they do love God with all their heart, when (alas) they know not the power of these things upon their own souls, thy heart is naturally a liar, and therefore believe it not. Thus the Pharisees did not know their own hearts, when they prayed, fasted and gave alms: Thus the Jews did not know their own hearts, when they cried *The Temple of the Lord*, and abounded in Sacrifices. This knowing of our own hearts is a supernatural lesson, taught only by the Spirit of God. Oh this self-flattery, how doth it damn its thousands, men making it no question, but they do repent and love God, when yet Christ hath said, *Many are called, but few chosen,* that is, of those many that are called by God to the enjoyment of the Church Ordinances and Priviledges, few have those true works of grace, which are proper to the elect only. O how should this terrible sentence spoken by Christ himself, make thee question again and again, yes a thousand times again, whether thou art called only, and no more, no chosen at all, for they are few.[38]

So we see that, while Burgess considers the discernment of signs to be the surest and most objective and reliable path to distinguishing true and false assurance, he also sees its dangers and gives various warnings

35. Ibid., 58–59.
36. Ibid., 57.
37. Ibid., 56.
38. Ibid., 57–58.

and caveats for approaching the evidence and deducing conclusions from it. Even as he extols the benefits and necessities of using signs to distinguish true and false assurance and affirms the possibility of making such distinctions, he also warns of self-flattery and self-love, that failing to look to the signs outlined in the word of God, an individual might turn inward to his or her sinful heart instead.

Goodwin and Owen on False Assurance

Just as we looked at Burgess's view of attaining assurance and compared and contrasted it with that of Goodwin and Owen in the previous chapter, so it will be worthwhile to do that in our study of false assurance, or presumption. For Goodwin, what we will see is that false assurance is not the primary category he discusses; rather, in Goodwin's case, temporary faith answers many of the same kinds of pastoral questions as those raised by presumption. For Owen, we will see a framework similar to Goodwin's, though bearing a few of the marks of Burgess's more developed theories regarding presumption.

Thomas Goodwin and Temporary Faith

The notion of temporary faith in Goodwin addresses roughly the same pastoral questions as does false assurance for Burgess. It provides an explanation for how it is possible for an individual to truly feel and even in some measure appear to have a saving interest in Jesus Christ yet not be truly among the saved. This phenomenon was identified by Burgess as presumption on the part of the individual, a false assurance borne of insufficient attention to the sins of genuine assurance. For Goodwin, it was a sign of temporary faith, a category he both defines and explains how to diagnose.

Temporary faith describes the state of someone who has truly believed but, as in the parable of the sower and the seed, had that faith choked out by the world and its cares. The Canons of the Synod of Dort make this point:

> That the faith of those who believe only temporarily does not differ from justifying and saving faith except in duration alone. For Christ himself in Matthew 13 20ff and Luke 8 13ff clearly defines these further differences between temporary and true believers he says the former receive the seed on rocky ground, and the latter receive it in good ground, or a good heart, the former have no root, and the latter are firmly rooted, the former have no fruit, and the latter produce fruit in varying measure, with steadfastness, or perseverance.[39]

This is exactly the language that Goodwin employs and seems to be just what he had in mind. It is possible for an individual to believe but to have a faith that is not a persevering faith, meaning it is no true faith at all. Only persevering faith saves. This could lead to a situation where someone makes what appears to be—and in a sense is—a credible profession of faith in Christ, only later to turn away or face the gravest doubts. Although both Burgess and Goodwin affirm the possibility of temporary faith being the explanation for such a state of affairs, Goodwin uses this as the primary explanation, where Burgess employs the language of presumption.

When considering the question of how one gains assurance, we have seen that Goodwin offers as his primary answer the advice of reflecting internally on the specific activities and personalities of each person in the triune godhead. The believer is to reflect on the nature of God as Father, for instance; Goodwin believes this reflection will increase the measure of the believer's assurance. In the case of temporary faith, Goodwin essentially explains the nature of

---

39. Canons of the Synod of Dordt, fifth point, rejection 7. Accessed online at http://kproj.com/KprojLibrary/Our Confessions of Faith/The Canons of Dort.pdf

the problem in terms of the individual misunderstanding or lacking appreciation for the true nature of God and God's salvation.

For instance, Goodwin sees that the individual could very well be understanding the Holy Spirit simply as a sovereign ruler, not as a redeemer.[40] This misunderstanding explains the problem of the false teachers in 2 Pet. 2:1. They saw God simply as a sovereign to whom they owed much, rather than as a merciful savior and heavenly father. They related to God as slaves relate to masters, not as sons to fathers. While this kind of "believer" might obey and serve God for some time, the manner of his or her appreciation for God resembles that of the covenant of works, rather than the covenant of grace.[41] These temporary believers may pretend to be God's sons; they may even obey God's laws, but they have not truly apprehended them. They feel in constant danger of being discovered by the law of God, which to them is the source of their salvation.[42]

Because these temporary believers have never understood their relationship with God properly, Goodwin also concludes that they have never understood the nature of God properly either. True believers will apprehend not only the holiness and purity and justice of God, but also God's goodness and grace.[43] They are approaching God first as a God of grace and goodness.

The difficulty, of course, is that temporary believers may show many signs of obedience to God's law and may even feel its convicting power and transformative effect on behavior. The conscience of a temporary believer may be stirred to action, but it is still relating to God from a perspective of works righteousness.[44]

---

40. Thomas Goodwin, *The Works of Thomas Goodwin.* 12 vols, Nichol's Series of Standard Divines. Puritan Period. (Edinburgh: J. Nichol, 1861), 6:56–58.
41. Ibid., 6:57.
42. Ibid., 6:328.
43. Ibid., 6:142.
44. Ibid., 6:240.

As for the temporary believer's apprehension of Christ himself, Horton summarizes Goodwin's perspective well: "It should be noted, therefore, that for Goodwin, the emphasis in distinguishing temporary from persevering faith falls not on outward signs or evidences so much as on whether the object is Christ as he is offered in the covenant of grace. Goodwin is most vitally concerned to point people to Christ directly, not to point them to assurance, nor to evidences, nor to graces, but to Christ, 'nakedly and barely considered' as the justifier of the godly."[45]

There is an aspect of this question that Goodwin does address with a slightly greater appeal to evidences. That comes when he is considering this doctrine negatively; that is, he goes into greater detail about evidence when discussing what temporary faith *is not*. This, of course, has direct bearing on the question of assurance. Essentially, Goodwin is attempting to comfort and inform true believers who may question whether or not their faith is temporary faith.

Here Goodwin wants to disabuse believers of several notions they may have about their own spiritual status. He wants them to understand, for instance, that temporary faith cannot be identified by observing the decline in one's own spiritual affections. He writes:

> So hath every regenerate man a world of thorns in him ay (says Calvin), thick-set corpses of them. Every one's grace is sown and continues amongst a wood of thorns. Yea, but yet there is another root of something that grows up in thy heart, that is not thorns, and there is a conflict against the thorns, an endeavor to stub them up, and they are thorns in thy side. Therefore, there is another principle in thee. *Obj 2* Thou wilt again say: I do not grow by reason of these thorns. But comfort thyself (says Calvin), for he that brought forth the thirty-fold is

45. Michael Horton, "Thomas Goodwin and the Puritan Doctrine of Assurance: Continuity and Discontinuity in the Reformed Tradition, 1600–1680" (PhD diss., Wycliffe Hall, Oxford and University of Coventry, 1999), 334.

by Christ reckoned with him that brought forth the hundred-fold. *Obj 3* But you will object, Alas my affections were mightily flushed at first, and now they wither, and worldly lusts grow up in their stead. *Ans* Shall I yet say to thee, Doth God maintain a conflict in thee against sin, an endeavor to stub up the thorns? Dost thou water those roots of bitterness with bitter tears and sorrow, and with the blood of Christ, to kill them? Then still the root of the matter remains in thee. Again, consider when thou wert first converted to God, as thou hadst grace in thee, so thou wert a temporary believer at first, as well as what was truly gracious, and when all was stirred, there must needs be a great flush of affection.

At first, half thy heart, thy unregenerate part, was turned a temporary believer too, and self-love, the great Simon Magus in thee, was wrought upon, and became a temporary believer, but yet besides, and over and beyond that, there was a little fountain opened in thy heart, and this continues still to flow, when the land-flood ceases, and then look, what is true grace indeed holds out the conduct against itself in worldly lusts, and bears alone the stress of all, and then worldly lusts begin to content purely with this little grace in us, and that fights it out alone, and then is the truer trial of grace, though less discernable to sense than it was at first.[46]

This is how Goodwin argues. He is not intending to discern true and temporary faith (or real assurance and false presumption) by their respective results, and he is certainly not trying to plant the seed of doubt in the minds of true Christians. As Horton writes, "Goodwin insists that God does not reject the temporary believer because of a lack of works or because the faith was not 'fully formed' by charity (as in Rome's view), but precisely because he or she is trusting in these attainments of the flesh."[47] Goodwin puts the issue this way:

For they will never come off to receive God and his grace upon his own terms, nor set up God's banners of his free grace to them, and of sincere love to him, upon their turrets above self, and so by degrees the Lord

---

46. Goodwin, *Works*, 6:345.
47. Horton, "Goodwin and Assurance," 338.

withdraws his treaties from them, and they by degrees become revolters from him, and in the end return to some of their own rebellions, upon which God says, 'Which covenant and treaty they brake, and I regarded them not' . . . . God hereby makes way to confound the corrupt doctrinal opinions that men have of grace. All Pelagian, semi-Pelagian and Jesuitical doctrines and all Arminian tenets about converting grace, have in their several proportions arisen from what men in their own experience have taken to be true workings of grace in their souls, or else from the pride of carnal wisdom, whereby men of learning and parts think to understand this.[48]

There can be little question that the approach Goodwin takes to the question of presumption differs from that of Burgess. This is not to say they would have disagreed with each other, but it is to say they did not approach the presenting problem from the same angle. Goodwin, seeing the problem of those who seemed certain of their saving faith, introduces the possibility of temporary faith, whereas Burgess addresses it from the standpoint of false assurance or presumption.

Perhaps because of these initial differences in approach, Burgess and Goodwin place the accent in decidedly different places. Burgess goes to great lengths to show the distinguishing marks of true assurance and contrasts these with things that either mark false assurance or else are no marks at all. Burgess intends for individuals to reason backward, looking at the true evidences carefully and distinguishing from these whether or not assurance is warranted. But because Goodwin believes that all the outward and many of the inward marks of true faith can accompany temporary faith as well, he points us in a different direction. Temporary faith does not differ in its outworking as much as in its manner of approach. It evidences conviction by the word of God, fealty to God (at least for a time), and obedience to God's law. What it does not do is approach God

48. Goodwin, *Works*, 6:332.

as the giver of grace and the only source of salvation. Its manner of attaining conviction, fealty, and obedience is centered on good works.

While it is entirely possible (even likely) that Goodwin and Burgess would not have strongly disagreed with the other's explicit statements, it is undeniable that the way they addressed the situation differed sharply. Both were in agreement with the consensus on faith and assurance reached at Westminster. Both were attempting to follow the framework of the WCF to its logical pastoral conclusions. And both were faced with the problem of discerning true professions of faith and distinguishing true claims of assurance from false ones. Further, in both, we see a decidedly pastoral interest in affirming and supporting the faith of true Christians who at times doubted their saving interest in Christ. But while one attempted to navigate this terrain by means of a turn inward, focusing on the approach to God and discounting in large measure the good works that might or might not be on display, the other believed that the actions and attitudes of the individual are the clearest key to unlocking the veracity of his or her claims to an assured faith.

John Owen on False Assurance

John Owen, like Burgess and Goodwin, agreed with the WCF about the possibility of false assurance. Even more than that, he believed that the possibility of false assurance posed a great danger to the church and to the individual. Those in a false state of assurance regarding their salvation are in fact the worst kind of individuals in terms of their relationship with God. He writes, "There are none in the world that deal worse with God than those who have an ungrounded persuasion of forgiveness."[49]

At the same time, Owen recognized that there might in fact be many believers who, though they are truly saved, are so moved and awed by the justice of God that they lose their sense of assurance or struggle to gain it at all. There are three causes of this lack of assurance, even where it is warranted: conscience, God's law, and a person's sense of God's justice.[50] The sensitive conscience can be moved to doubt because of the continuing presence of sin; Owen sees the conscience opposed to the notion *by its very nature:* "[The conscience] knows nothing of forgiveness; yea, it is against its very trust, work, and office to hear anything of it."[51] He also writes of conscience, "Conscience, if not seared, inexorably condemneth and pronounceth wrath and anger upon the soul that hath the least guilt cleaving to it. Now, it hath this advantage, it lieth close to the soul, and by importunity and loud speaking it will be heard in what it hath to say; it will make the whole soul attend, or it will speak like thunder. And its constant voice is, that where there is guilt there must be judgment."[52]

An understanding of God's law can also work against the notion of assurance, since it too knows nothing of forgiveness or mercy. In this, the conscience and the law of God are in full agreement, arguing against any hope or assurance of God's forgiving mercy.[53] Owen writes, "The very sanction of it lies wholly against them: 'The soul that sinneth, it shall die.'"[54] And of the law's work within a person's inner being, he writes:

It came into the world with him, and hath grown up with him from his infancy. It was implanted in his heart by nature, — is his own reason;

49. John Owen, *The Works of John Owen.* 16 vols (Edinburgh: Banner of Truth, 1965), 6:396.
50. Sinclair Ferguson, *John Owen on the Christian Life* (Edinburgh: Banner of Truth, 1995), 101.
51. Owen, *Works*, 6:387.
52. Ibid., 6:387.
53. Ibid., 6:389.
54. Ibid.

he can never shake it off or part with it. It is his familiar, his friend, that cleaves to him as the flesh to the bone; so that they who have not the law written cannot but show forth the work of the law, Romans 2:14, 15, and that because the law itself is inbred to them. And all the faculties of the soul are at peace with it, in subjection to it. It is the bond and ligament of their union, harmony, and correspondency among themselves, in all their moral actings. It gives life, order, motion to them all.[55]

In addition to these two causes, which themselves are knit together, comes people's innate sense of the justice of God. The true notion of God's total justice naturally leads to despair about the possibility of forgiveness:

There are in all men by nature indelible characters of the holiness and purity of God, of his justice and hatred of sin, of his invariable righteousness in the government of the world, that they can neither depose nor lay aside; for notions of God, whatever they are, will bear sway and role in the heart, when things are put to the trial. They were in the heathens of old; they abode with them in all their darkness; as might be manifested by innumerable instances. But so it is in all men by nature. Their inward thought is, that God is an avenger of sin; that it belongs to his rule and government of the world, his holiness and righteousness, to take care that every sin be punished; this is his judgment, which all men know, as was observed before, Romans 1:32. They know that it is a righteous thing with God to render tribulation unto sinners. From thence is that dread and fear which surpriseth men at an apprehension of the presence of God, or of any thing under him, above them, that may seem to come on his errand. This notion of God's avenging all sin exerts itself secretly but effectually. So Adam trembled, and hid himself. And it was the saying of old, 'I have seen God, and shall die.' When men are under any dreadful providence, — thunderings, lightnings, tempests, in darkness, — they tremble; not so much at what they see, or hear, or feel, as from their secret thoughts that God is nigh, and that he is a consuming fire.

Now, these inbred notions lie universally against all apprehensions of

---

55. Ibid.

forgiveness, which must be brought into the soul from without doors, having no principle of nature to promote them.[56]

With all these impediments to genuine assurance, where does Owen see false assurance creeping in? In fact, Owen sees the possibility of false assurance arising precisely because of all the impediments to genuine assurance. Individuals may be persuaded by some means to ignore the witness of their conscience, or of the law of God, or of their general sense of God's justice, and may genuinely believe that God is now predisposed toward them in mercy and forgiveness. The problem is that such individuals may not feel assured of God's positive predisposition, but may misunderstand totally the nature of God's actual mechanism for forgiveness through the death of Jesus Christ. Essentially what the individual is doing is presuming on God's forbearance, not trusting in God's Son.[57] Ferguson summarizes Owen's thinking this way:

> Men think that God is not really just and holy in the way the Scripture teaches, but, recreating him in their own image, imagine him to be like themselves. This error is reinforced by their vague sense that God is willing to forgive, without taking account of *the way* in which God forgives. It is a cardinal principle in Owen's though that genuine acceptance of the gospel and all its benefits requires an *approval* of the gospel method of justification. The method of grace is that a *righteous* and *holy* God forgives. This is the heart of the gospel. It is also the paradox at the heart of the gospel, resolved only in Christ. It is one thing, therefore, to have a vague hope of forgiveness, another to discover that there is forgiveness with the true and living God.[58]

What this kind of misunderstanding leads to is a false sense of assurance. One becomes certain that God's disposition is changed, but sees the change as either a change in God's essential character

56. Ibid., 6:391.
57. Ibid., 6:393.
58. Ferguson, *John Owen on the Christian Life*, 101.

and disposition (from judging sin by the law to forgiving it) apart from Christ, or as a change brought about by one's own reform or repentance. In either case, whatever such an individual feels about God, he or she has misunderstood the means by which God gives salvation to sinners. The person's conviction and assurance are grounded in an unwarranted presumption.

As we have seen in the previous chapter, Owen, like Goodwin, encouraged those who were seeking assurance to meditate on the Persons of the triune God. Only in fellowship with each does one become fully assured of the salvation offered and received through Jesus Christ. In light of this, it is perhaps no surprise that Owen diagnoses the main problem with false assurance as a failure to rightly understand the nature of the gospel's message regarding the mechanism by which God's disposition changes toward the sinner.

Although it is not the major focus of his writing on assurance, Owen does give some diagnostic advice about discerning true and false assurance. First, he writes that false presumption, as opposed to that which is genuine, arises without any difficulty on the part of those who receive it. Their easy reception indicates mere presumption. He writes, "They have not, by the power of their convictions and distresses of conscience, been put to make inquiry whether this thing be so or no. It is not a persuasion that they have arrived unto in a way of seeking satisfaction to their own souls. It is not the result of a deep inquiry after peace and rest. It is antecedent unto trial and experience, and so is not faith, but opinion."[59] In essence, one distinguishing mark of true assurance is the difficulty with which it is achieved. True assurance comes only after trials and difficulties, after careful and diligent searching.

59. Owen, *Works*, 6:395.

Owen also says that the effect of false assurance is quite different from that which accompanies genuine assurance. Here he begins to approach the method and conclusions of Burgess in the matter, though Burgess gives far more attention to the topic. Essentially, Owen argues that true assurance—a sure and certain knowledge of God's forgiveness in Christ—creates in the believer a more genuine reverence of and love for God. Or to put it in the negative, false assurance leads to a flippant or casual view of God. He writes, "Carnal boldness, formality, and despising of God, are the common issues of such a notion and persuasion. Indeed, this is the generation of great sinners in the world; men who have a general apprehension, but not a sense of the special power of pardon, openly or secretly, in fleshly or spiritual sins, are the great sinners among men. Where faith makes a discovery of forgiveness, all things are otherwise. Great love, fear, and reverence of God, are its attendants. Mary Magdalene loved much, because much was forgiven."[60]

In addition to the attitude toward God that false assurance breeds, it also brings about an inappropriate attitude toward sin. Whereas real assurance brings hatred and revulsion at sin, recognizing the price that Christ paid to appease the Father's wrath on account of it, false assurance is marked by a cavalier attitude toward one's sin. So wretched is this condition, in which an offer of forgiveness—misunderstood and unapplied—leads to sin, that Owen writes, "It would be well for many if they had never heard the name of forgiveness."[61]

Finally, Owen indicates that a general notion of forgiveness or a false assurance of salvation does not bring true rest to the heart in the end: "Flashes of joy it may, abiding rest it doth not."[62] In the

60. Ibid., 6:396.
61. Ibid., 6:397.
62. Ibid.

end, the mark of false assurance is a tossing up and down within the soul. Depending on one's behavior, assurance comes and goes. Since this false assurance is based on a false view of God to begin with, it constantly looks to the person's fluctuating heart, finding in it no rest at all.

Conclusion

Both Goodwin and Owen, contemporaries of Anthony Burgess, affirmed the possibility envisioned in the WCF concerning false assurance. They both understood that there was a very real possibility that someone could make a claim to have assurance when in fact that claim was nothing more than presumption. In that sense, they held all the same presuppositions on the subject as Burgess. But there were differences as well.

One of the chief ways in which Owen and Goodwin differ from Burgess is the sheer volume of teaching Burgess gives on the topic of presumption. Compared with Burgess, Goodwin and Owen provide a relative paucity of teaching on the topic, though both of them do address it as a possibility in their broader discussions of true assurance.

But the differences go far deeper. Burgess, for instance, gives a great deal of attention to the role that the preached word can play in dividing true assurance from mere presumption. In fact, for Burgess, this is one of the main roles of preaching within the church, especially for those claiming some kind of salvation. The preacher, in confronting hearers with the living Christ and in showcasing the glories of union with Christ, exposes that which is false in the heart of the hearers. This emphasis on the role of preaching, which we find both in our examination of Burgess's treatise on assurance and in our broader investigation of his description of pastoral ministry, sets

Burgess's expansions upon the Westminster consensus on assurance apart from those of his contemporaries.

Perhaps even more striking is the difference in the kinds of evidence that each relies upon. Burgess relies only very slightly on the kind of internal, subjective marks of false assurance appealed to by Goodwin and, to a lesser extent, by Owen. Instead, he provides what he considers to be more objective, external marks of true assurance and of false assurance. His aim is to give both ministers and individual Christians the tools for reasoning backward. As they look at the evidences provided in their own lives or in the lives of those to whom they minister, they are able to conclude from these evidences something of the status of the individual's profession of assurance.

This seems to run counter to the emphasis of Owen and directly contradicts some of the statements made by Goodwin. Goodwin, rather than discussing false assurance, instead deals with the whole question under the broader heading of temporary faith. The problem for Goodwin is that temporary faith bears outward fruit that is precisely the same as that of true faith, so reasoning backward from the presence of certain marks or signs is, for him, a futile and potentially deceptive exercise. Burgess disagrees, arguing that the marks of genuine assurance do differ in quality and kind from those produced by temporary faith or false assurance. Owen is perhaps the mediating figure in this. What little time he spends on false assurance tends toward the same inward-looking direction as Goodwin follows, and many of the same problems with temporary faith, so clearly outlined by Goodwin, are echoed in Owen's discussion of false assurance. But there is also in Owen an acknowledgment that the fruit of these inward misunderstandings and misappropriations of the work of Christ will also lead to a different kind of outward life. The attitude of the presumptuous person will be different, as will the person's attitude toward sin and the quality of his or her love. All these marks serve the same kind of diagnostic, objective, evidentiary purpose as those discussed in Burgess's treatise, though they are outlined in far less detail.

Burgess's approach to false assurance or presumption is in keeping with his general approach to the topic of assurance. While Owen and Goodwin seek to tease out internal and more subjective evidences, Burgess seems to rely on that which is more concrete. In leading individuals to a fully formed assurance, he instructs them to look to the ways in which God is working in them in a manner consistent with salvation. In the matter of false assurance, he does the same. The fruits of presumption are, in his estimation, quite different from those produced by a genuine assurance.

Conclusion

My concern in this book has been to demonstrate that the divergent views of assurance, so notable in the later Scottish tradition and so often remarked upon when comparing Calvin with the English Puritans, have much deeper, more complex roots than previously imagined. We have seen first that the Westminster Assembly was designed to foster broad consensus from the beginning, making the Westminster Confession of Faith (WCF) essentially a consensus document. Although some have imagined the WCF as a kind of scholastic straitjacket or a revolutionary set of theological innovations (especially on the question of assurance), in fact its areas of emphasis and explanation on the matter of assurance appear to have been relatively uncontroversial.

But the peculiar fact remains that immediately after the WCF statement on assurance was codified, there emerged at least two streams of interpretation, broadly represented in this study by the work of Anthony Burgess on the one hand, and Thomas Goodwin and John Owen on the other. The question of what those divergent streams represented was the subject of the main body of our study.

The question of why these streams were so divergent is much harder to answer. In most respects, the broad social and educational background of our three major characters is similar. They were all identifiable as Puritans (despite the difficulties with this term); they were all pastors who saw their work through the lens of pastoral practice; they were all trained in an educational environment that might be broadly termed Scholastic (though this term is fraught with difficulties of its own). And perhaps most importantly, all of these men would have happily agreed with the Westminster consensus statement on assurance. Yet against the backdrop of this broad similarity, we can begin to see differences that would define the later history of the doctrine of assurance.

Importance of the Topic

The importance of the doctrine of assurance is based on several factors. First, the question of how someone might truly know he or she was saved—and, conversely, the ways in which persons might be deceived on this same question—was of undeniable significance in the context of the seventeenth-century English ecclesiastical scene. Indeed, as we have seen, both the nature of the Reformation reaction to Roman Catholicism and the increasingly strong pastoral needs of the Puritans made the subject of assurance one of considerable importance. Not surprisingly, it also was important in the context of the Westminster Assembly. This is what we would expect, given its overall significance in church life at the time. What is surprising is the degree to which unanimity existed among those responsible for the formulations of the WCF.

The topic was also one to which Anthony Burgess, Thomas Goodwin, and John Owen each made a distinctive contribution. Examining these contributions is helpful for two particular reasons. First, it gives us a better overall understanding of the key streams of Reformed *pastoral* thinking on the subject. But second, it provides a test case for examining our overall understanding of the varying ways in which the WCF was understood and expanded upon, even among those who were responsible for its writing. That is, it enables us to see how the first generation of pastors following the WCF expanded on its consensus statement in important ways. As they recognized its inadequacy in addressing the pastoral needs they faced, they filled in the gaps in the WCF. It is especially noteworthy that they filled in these gaps in different ways; Anthony Burgess, as we have seen, fills in the silences of the WCF in much different ways than Thomas Goodwin and John Owen. But it should be noted that all three considered themselves firm adherents to the Westminster consensus, and two of them—Goodwin and Burgess—actually participated in the assembly itself. Therefore, examining Burgess in comparison with these others provides us with a remarkable window into the process of development that occurred quite rapidly after the English Puritan consensus of the WCF was codified.

Evaluation of Various Approaches to Assurance

From a practical perspective, it would seem that there are significant flaws in the approach of the WCF itself toward assurance, and in the approaches of Burgess, Owen, and Goodwin. The WCF does not provide more than a bare framework for understanding the topic. This is not necessarily a failure in the document. After all, it was never intended to be a pastoral manual, and the assembly, though made up of pastors, had an entirely different mandate for its work. Nonetheless, the fact that such significant expansion was obviously necessary in the immediate aftermath of its writing indicates that more could have been said.

In Burgess's case, we see that his writings on the matter of assurance have many strong features but also several weaknesses. First, he expands on the Westminster consensus significantly. While the mandate of the assembly was not to compose a pastoral treatise, Burgess saw this as part of his pastoral calling. The fact that he expanded so comprehensively shows us something about the silences of the WCF, but it is also a step forward pastorally. In addition, Burgess is to be commended for the clear role he assigns to preaching in the quest for assurance. Both the preaching of the word and the overall life of the congregation play a significant part in Burgess's understanding of how one achieves and maintains assurance. In that sense, he is far less individualistic than either Goodwin or Owen in his approach to the topic. Since the WCF also envisions assurance to be a possibility for someone in the context of the right and necessary means of grace, it can also be said that Burgess is closer to the WCF in this respect than Goodwin and Owen appear to be. Finally, it should be noted that Burgess does not spend nearly as much time as Goodwin and Owen on contemplating what Goodwin terms the intuitive means of assurance. Because of this, I would argue that he is far more constructive and concrete than either Goodwin or Owen manages to be. So Burgess's writings, in their comprehensiveness, general ecclesiastical focus, and concrete and discursive analysis, must be commended highly.

Burgess's discursive analysis also appears to have significant flaws. In the first place, his writings could tend toward a kind of legalism, focused as they are on outward manifestations that, in his thinking, demonstrate to an individual his or her status before God. But also, Burgess's analysis of the signs of true assurance are still quite subjective, a fact that becomes clear when he begins to address the question of presumption. In the end, it becomes quite impossible for Burgess to speak with precision about the quality, depth, or duration of particular signs required for them to be dispositive in a particular case. So although he strives to be objective and concrete, there is still an element of subjectivity in the whole process.

When we take up Goodwin and Owen, we see that their writings, too, ultimately could lead to a large measure of subjectivity, though for an additional reason. Their focus is not on a discursive analysis of the signs of true conversion, but rather of the inward and subjective pursuit of assurance through a vital communion with the triune God. In fact, Goodwin—the more extreme of the two in this matter—positively rejects the notion of looking for outward concrete signs, instead opting for what he calls an "intuitive" understanding of assurance. This seems merely to compound the problem of subjectivity for those pursuing assurance, since now one not only has to look at works to try to discern whether they are ample and telling, but also to look at an inward experience, one that Goodwin and Owen themselves concede can come and go. Added to this is Goodwin's particular notion of the sealing of the Spirit (rejected by Owen) as an additional spiritual experience after true conversion.

In addition to the charge of a measure of subjectivity, which it seems none of them ultimately avoid, there is also the matter of an individualistic focus. Burgess comes nearest to avoiding this, since he often refers to the importance of the local congregation, and particularly the pastor, in helping Christians gain assurance and in convicting those who are living in presumption. But even Burgess, with his ecclesiological focus, deals with assurance as ultimately an individual issue. This appears to be a move away from the WCF conception, which focused on the ordinary means—prayer, sacraments, and the preached word—as providing assurance. Goodwin and Owen have an even greater individualistic focus. For them, assurance seems to be an entirely private matter, in which the individual wrestles and struggles with internal experiences that may wax and wane. Surely this could not help but foster some moments of agonizing self-doubt about the reality of one's saving faith, which seems far removed from the statements of certainty found and anticipated by believers in the New Testament itself.

Specific Conclusions

After surveying the theological landscape prior to Westminster, we then turned to a description of the work of the Westminster Assembly. Recent scholarly efforts enable us to view the Westminster Assembly in a clearer light than before. We have more reliable records and more insightful analysis of its procedures than we have had. These records and this analysis show how the Westminster Assembly operated in practice. In effect, the assembly was built for consensus. This is not a criticism. In fact, it may well have been a strength of its work, but it serves to underscore the degree to which its conclusions might well omit significant areas that were disputed or controversial or else deemed to be too specific and narrow for the assembly to comment upon. Demonstrating this feature of the assembly's work has brought to light emphases from very recent areas of scholarly research and has utilized the materials of as-yet unpublished historical materials.

This analysis of the overall goals of the Westminster Assembly led to some observations about the specific formulations of the WCF regarding assurance. We saw that the formulations, which in themselves have often raised questions of continuity with earlier Reformed traditions, in this case raised few, if any, questions for those who assembled at Westminster. That is, the WCF defined the matter of assurance in ways that were seemingly uncontroversial, at least for those who participated in the deliberations of the assembly. Indeed, as we have argued, this was part of the point for the Westminster Assembly. It was designed to reach a consensus, and it succeeded in doing so. This is not to say there were not heated and important debates in the assembly; it has been well documented that there were, especially in the area of ecclesiology. But the essential approach was one that gave the greatest possibility of consensus, at least among those who had been invited to participate. In any case, we can certainly see that the question of assurance was hardly debated, and the statement that came out of Westminster was a consensus statement about which there was little apparent disagreement.

Yet as we have examined the statement carefully, we see that its broadly agreeable consensus statement leaves some significant questions unanswered. While it acknowledges that assurance is possible, it does not say precisely *how* it is possible. It remained for the pastors who followed to work through this question.

Further, the WCF did introduce with some detail the fact that someone could be deceived about assurance. That is, one could be engaged in a kind of presumption about one's own standing with Christ. The WCF even goes into some detail about how all this might be possible. But it does not give any kind of pastoral detail about how one can discern whether or not one's assurance of faith is truly genuine or is merely presumptuous. Again, it would fall to others to expand upon this in ways that would serve the particular needs of their pastoral callings.

My second contention is that, in order to understand the nature of various contributions to the doctrine of assurance after Westminster, one must first begin to understand each contributor's associations, vocation, and education. First, each of the men we considered was a Puritan. While there is still no scholarly consensus on how that term should best be used, it does still, in my opinion, have some value. It does seem to be useful historical shorthand for a group of people who identified with each other at the time as having certain core convictions and a resistance to specific tendencies within the established church. What is especially important to remember is that this moniker is not simply a later construct, imposed back on a few figures who fit its arbitrary definition. Rather, it was a term used at the time, and it identifies a group of people who would themselves have identified with one another. It is this historical anchoring that makes the term not only useful but legitimate in referring to a movement within the seventeenth century.

Second, I argued that it is necessary to take into account the position each of these men held as a pastor. While Burgess had the opportunity, because of a change in the guidelines of his college, to continue living the life of an academic don, he chose instead to begin work as a pastor. He remained committed to his congregation at Sutton Coldfield even through ejections and persecutions, and while in London as part of the Westminster Assembly, he still managed to lead and even undertake reforms at the church in St. Lawrence Jewry. Goodwin, as we have seen, was involved in pastoral ministry from the earliest days after his conversion; indeed, his adult life was characterized by extensive pastoral ministry. Owen's pastoral work, though in some ways less grounded in one location, was nonetheless extensive. He was both a chaplain and a pastor throughout much of the time during which he wrote.

What I have contended is that this pastoral context explains at least two of the aspects of Burgess's, Goodwin's and Owen's expansions on the Westminster doctrine of assurance. First, the pastoral context created the drive for Burgess, Goodwin, Owen, and others to expand on the gaps left in the WCF. That is, as pastors consumed with matters of pastoral significance, they could not (and did not) simply allow the ambiguities in the WCF statement on assurance to go unresolved. Instead, each would need to undertake a program to fill in those gaps. They added much fuller and more comprehensive statements to the distilled essence of the Westminster formulation. And they did this not because of a fundamental disagreement with the basic emphases of the WCF (it appears they did not differ with it), but rather because their pastoral contexts, and the pastoral context of so many with whom they associated, demanded it. To fail to understand these men as pastors is to be unable to grasp the prime reason behind their expansion on the Westminster consensus. By this, we mean not only that they expanded on the WCF because of their pastoral needs, but also that they did so in ways that did not directly address certain specific questions related to covenant theology, the extent of the atonement, or the nature of God's decrees. To be sure, they were aware of these debates and important distinctions, but what we find in their treatises is the distilled essence of their conclusions as they were to be applied to pastors, congregations, individual Christians, and those who claimed to have saving faith.

Second, the ways in which these three men filled in the WCF were decidedly practical and concrete. Burgess generally avoided turning individuals to an introspective and mystical pursuit of assurance of saving faith, but rather turned them toward more concrete and external means of assurance, emphasizing throughout the ecclesiastical context in which assurance must be pursued. And although Goodwin and Owen were slightly more introspective in their focus, they still attempted to give concrete instructions, even if what they were pointing toward was necessarily inward and abstract.

Finally, we have argued that in order to understand the distinctive contribution of each of these men, it is important to understand them in light of their particular educational background. To establish this, we went into some detail explaining the kind of schooling Burgess, Goodwin, and Owen received, from pre-undergraduate education up through university and even beyond. Each of these educational steps prepared these men in specific ways for the kind of theological project they were to undertake. More importantly, when we look at the finished product of their theological work, we can see quite clearly the evidence of their educational background.

This seems especially true of Burgess and his use of syllogisms. It is not, as some have claimed, that Burgess's Scholastic training forced him into certain theological abstractions. Rather, I would argue, his pastoral vocation made him expand on the question of assurance in more detailed ways, but his Scholastic training, particularly in the area of syllogistic reasoning and argumentation, did provide the raw materials for how he argued his theological conclusions. That is, I am saying that the questions he raised were primarily demanded by his pastoral setting, but the method in which he answered them often bore great resemblance to the scholastic environment in which he was educated. He was unafraid to use syllogistic reasoning to prove his point about assurance; in fact, he seems to have gravitated toward it.

The interesting detail to note here is the way in which Burgess differed from Goodwin and Owen both in the method of pursuing assurance and in his mode of argumentation. I have argued that Burgess's discourse bears the mark of his Scholastic training, and indeed it seems that it would be hard to understand his syllogistic framework apart from that. Yet Goodwin and Owen arose out of a similar educational milieu, and their discussion of assurance does not seem to bear these same marks. Two things can be said about this. First, while I have argued that Burgess is a product of his training, this is not the same as arguing that his training inexorably led to his argumentation. That is, Burgess's education may have been a necessary condition for his later work, but in itself, it is not sufficient to explain the work. So another theologian, having received much the same training as Burgess, might well—and did, in point of fact—argue differently.

Second, it should be noted that Burgess's Scholastic training went beyond instruction in the syllogisms. In fact, while this goes considerably beyond the scope of this book, aspects of Goodwin and Owen are characteristic of this training; these include the careful attention to distinctions and definitions that are only inferred in the text of Scripture, and the use of ancient languages and sources, among others. To explore the ways in which the Scholastic training of the early seventeenth century influenced all the Puritans would be a worthwhile yet monumental undertaking. I have contented myself with highlighting the distinctive ways in which Burgess employed the training he received and the ways in which that training was similar to, if not exactly the same as, Goodwin's and Owen's.

When we then examine these three men, we see that they did expand on the consensus reached at Westminster. They did so by clarifying the nature of true assurance and the way in which someone could attain and retain it. They also articulated the nature of presumption and the way in which an individual could discern between true assurance and false presumption. These expansions show the ways in which the post-Westminster theologians remained true to the consensus of the WCF while still expanding on this consensus in important and necessary ways. Comparing the three, we can see that the expansions were variegated, but we cannot reasonably question the fact that they were indeed expansions.

Also, Burgess's treatises give significantly—and perhaps uniquely—added attention to the corporate, or ecclesiastical, means of assuring oneself and, for that matter, of detecting presumption. Assurance is never considered apart from one's membership in a local church, and the ecclesiastical context must be considered when evaluating Burgess's contribution on assurance. Interestingly, this ecclesiastical element of assurance does not seem to have been considered by Owen, Goodwin, or the divines of Westminster.

In the future, it would be worth pursuing the ways in which this new understanding of the patterns of development from the Westminster Assembly, given what we can now say about its nature, might apply to other areas of doctrine in the seventeenth century, such as the church, the civil magistrate, and the sacraments. While assurance was a prime pastoral concern of the Puritan era in England, it was far from the only concern, and while there has been much discussion about the WCF formulation on assurance, this was by no means the only doctrinal issue that Westminster sought to address. In fact, while questions of continuity and discontinuity have often dominated the debates about seventeenth-century English theology, it might be worth extending the question to look not only at the streams of thought that converged in the WCF, as Robert Letham and Richard Muller have done, but also at the streams that developed *out of* the WCF, as theologians sought to remain faithful to their commitment to Westminster orthodoxy in the face of complex pastoral needs and various ideas about the exact implications of the statements made in the WCF.

Our study of assurance—using Anthony Burgess's writings as a starting point and contrasting them with the writings of others who shared his basic commitment to the WCF—may be seen as a first step in this larger area of study. What we have certainly concluded from this examination of one aspect of Westminster theology is that the Puritans—even those who directly contributed to and adopted the WCF—were by no means monolithic in their approach to theological questions. The WCF, arising as it did out of a context in which broad consensus was essential, left too many gaps for that. The ongoing nature of Puritan pastoral ministry, along with the need for more detailed and theologically precise formulations, contributed to this ongoing development. While we find among the English Puritans of the seventeenth century a broad consensus about the formulations of the WCF, we do not find their various expansions on the consensus to be identical at all; in fact, they seem to have very different implications and emphases. One suspects that this same pattern of diverging streams of thought would hold as true in other areas as it does in the area of assurance.

This phenomenon is somewhat like what chapter 2 observed regarding Reformed development prior to the seventeenth century, and it may be suggestive of a feature of the Reformed doctrine of assurance more generally. Among those who have largely similar notions and doctrinal loyalties, there are streams of thought that often take these notions in different directions. Sometimes this can be attributed to differences in pastoral need, sometimes to differences in the context of theological debate, and sometimes to real disagreements on fundamental matters. Whatever the reasons, divergent streams can be observed. From the perspective of historical research and theological labeling, it is often difficult to know when these streams are sufficiently divergent to call into question the basic consensus. In the case of Burgess, Owen, and Goodwin, it seems as if their consensus is deep enough for us to consider them part of the same general category, but the differences in approach to the matter of assurance are still significant enough to note, and must not be smoothed over artificially by those trying to retain certain historical categories in place. In the case of those following directly after Westminster, the issue is not Calvin versus the Calvinists (tired as that formulation may be); rather, it is the Westminster Calvinists versus the Westminster Calvinists! What we have seen is a diversity of views even in the first generation following the WCF formulation. It is perhaps a tribute to the robustness of these consensus formulations that, even though there were many variations among those who followed, there was an essential core, which remained solid enough to hold together the differing emphases and approaches.

The Puritans who contributed to the Westminster consensus and those who followed with their own expansions (often the same men) believed that individual Christian lives were powerfully affected by what they were taught regarding salvation, sin, presumption, and assurance. The streams of thought and application still seem to flow in different directions on this question, since, for many in the Reformed tradition, this commitment to the importance of assurance continues to be an animating conviction, with a variety of pastoral applications.

Index